Grimoire of a Kitchen Witch

An Essential Guide to Witchcraft

WHAT PEOPLE ARE SAYING ABOUT

GRIMOIRE OF A KITCHEN WITCH

This is certainly a very friendly book, providing a helpful guide to Kitchen Witchery and for those stepping onto the path, bringing practical spirituality back into the home.
Cat Treadwell, author of *A Druid's Tale*

I think if Terry Pratchett's witches wrote an introduction to magic, it would look a lot like this book. Pragmatic, playful, wise and sprinkled with humour, the author covers a lot of ground and isn't afraid to use a wooden spoon!
Nimue Brown, author of *Druidry & Meditation, Druidry & the Ancestors, & the Hopeless Maine Saga*

This book is packed with so much information that it makes you feel as though you have a major learning tool in your hands. Yet it is written in such a way that allows you to feel that the author is talking directly and personally to YOU! This conversational feel allows information to be passed on without any sense of preaching, dogma or ego. The writing style is friendly but also precise.

Although written from the kitchen witch perspective, this is a great book for all who follow an earthy path and as a shaman, I enjoyed it more than some of the shamanic books out there.

The book unfolds into more and more explanations, stories and advice without ever assuming knowledge but also never assuming that the reader is anything less than intelligent and sentient. So it is never preachy, starchy,condescending or obtuse.

I particularly enjoyed the sections on animal guides and

elementals. The meditations and lessons are well thought out and the little extras like Hoodoo and planetary influences are informative and fun. There is just so much packed into this book.
Colette Brown, author, Shaman & Clairvoyant Tarot Reader

Grimoire of a Kitchen Witch

An Essential Guide to Witchcraft

Rachel Patterson

MOON BOOKS

Winchester, UK
Washington, USA

First published by Moon Books, 2013
Moon Books is an imprint of John Hunt Publishing Ltd., Laurel House, Station Approach,
Alresford, Hants, SO24 9JH, UK
office1@jhpbooks.net
www.johnhuntpublishing.com
www.moon-books.net

For distributor details and how to order please visit the 'Ordering' section on our website.

ISBN: 978 1 78099 958 6

A CIP catalogue record for this book is available from the British Library.

Design: Stuart Davies

Printed and bound by CPI Group (UK) Ltd, Croydon, CR0 4YY

CONTENTS

Foreword: Who am I?

My craft name is Tansy Firedragon and I have been a witch for many years now, originally studying on my own as a solitary from books and the internet.

I then spent a year and a half studying and gaining a first degree with the Correllian Tradition of which I am an Outer Court Member. That was followed by nearly eight years studying for the Wiccan first, second and third degrees with two different groups and then becoming a High Priestess in 2011.

I studied with Janet Farrar and Gavin Bone on their Progressive Magick course, passing with a distinction. I have also studied druidry with the Order of Bards, Ovates and Druids, as well as tarot, the pendulum, herbalism, empathy, witches runes, hoodoo and aromatherapy. I have Reiki Level I and II attunements. In 2012 I was ordained as a Minister of the Universal Life Church.

I am High Priestess in my own coven co-run by my lovely sisters in the craft, the Kitchen Witch Coven of Natural Witchery as well as being a member of the Dorset Grove Druids, which allows me to attend lots of outside rituals in wonderful sacred places within the UK.

I am co-founder and a leadership team member of the online Kitchen Witch School of Natural Witchcraft; we also have a facebook page and a blog.

www.kitchenwitchhearth.com
www.kitchenwitchuk.blogspot.co.uk
www.facebook.com/kitchenwitchuk
Email: kitchenwitchhearth@yahoo.com

I have a personal blog www.tansyfiredragon.blogspot.co.uk
Personal email: tansyfiredragon@yahoo.com
My personal website: www.rachelpatterson.co.uk

My craft is a combination of old religion witchcraft, Wicca, kitchen witchery, green witchery and hoodoo. My heart is that of a kitchen witch. I am blessed with a wonderful husband, lovely children, a fabulous family and good friends.

My first book, Pagan Portals – Kitchen Witchcraft, was published in 2013 by Moon Books and my next book Pagan Portals Hoodoo will also be published later in 2013.

What is this book all about?

This book is essentially about my life and how I live and work as a kitchen witch. It is my Book of Shadows, my Kitchen Witch's Grimoire. It covers what it means to be a witch, how we work, what we do and how we celebrate the turning of the seasons. It is packed full of information about all sorts of subjects from a breakdown of rituals to reading auras, along with meditations, recipes for oils, incenses and spells and a huge amount of crafts to make for each Sabbat. The information herein does not follow any strict tradition; it is my own interpretation of witchcraft melding together my Wiccan training with kitchen witchery, ways of the Old Craft and a bit of hoodoo thrown in for good measure. You can also find a lot of information about magical cooking, herbs and gardening in my first book, Pagan Portals: Kitchen Witchcraft, it's not included here because I didn't want to duplicate!

I believe magic and the Craft to be fluid and flexible, it is ever changing and we are ever learning.

Chapter 1

What is a Witch?

The media would have everyone believe that a witch is a hunched over old hag with green skin, gnarled fingers and a wart on her nose. I have met a lot of witches and we come in all ages, shapes, sizes, colours (not green as far as I know) and all genders... but I have yet to meet one who looks like that.

I am hoping that in my crone years I will wear kaftans and floppy hats and be known locally as 'that mad ole witch' – not quite the Hollywood hag figure, but I am working on it.

What is a witch? Well to me a witch is someone who is in tune with the Earth, with the changing of the seasons, someone who connects with the elements and works with all the energies around them. I respect and care for the planet and all the plants and creatures that live on it and in it.

Witchcraft is a way of life; it is who I am, what I am and how I choose to live my life. It is a beautiful, rewarding and wonderful way of life.

It is a chosen path filled with self-discovery, learning, and growth as those who claim the title of witch will grow in knowledge and experiences for a lifetime and possibly more. Witchcraft is a generic term used to describe its many extensions and sub-categories.

There are no hard rules with witchcraft; you can tailor it to your personal beliefs, traditions and rituals.

Witchcraft is a polytheistic religion; this means there is more than one figurehead, a Goddess who has many names and a God who also goes by many names. I think of deity as being like the many facets of a diamond.

Witches all know and live with the God and the Goddess. They are both entities of the great All. Each witch carries a part of the God and Goddess within them. We respect them; work with them, live with them. However, to each of us the God and Goddess may be perceived differently.

The God is the male entity, the Sky Father, representative of the Sun. He goes by many names and many faces – Pan, Cernunnos, Osiris, Thor and Belenos to name a few.

The Goddess is the universal mother. She is representative of the Moon and the Earth. She, too, is known by many names and faces – Gaia, Hecate, Brighid, Cailleach, Kali to name a few.

They do not rule, but they do oversee; they are present, it is all according to your beliefs. They work together, forming a whole.

The true explanation of deity is within each witch's own heart. We reflect them with our daily intent and deeds.

Witches practice ritual observance of lunar events and the seasons. Rituals are split into two groups, Sabbats and Esbats. There are eight Sabbats in a year representing the cycle of birth and death of the God, these being Yule/Winter Solstice, Imbolc, Ostara, Beltane, Litha/Midsummer, Lughnasadh, Autumn Equinox (Mabon) and Samhain.

Esbats are Moon rituals, celebrating the New Moons and the Full Moons.

These rituals are performed within sacred or magic circles, and are used for the purposes of asking for guidance and giving thanks to the Goddess and God, and are often used for the performance of magic.

Some witches are members of a coven, in which there will be a High Priestess and/or High Priest. The other members will be witches of varying degrees of initiation. There are also many, many solitary witches. There are a large number of traditions within the witchcraft umbrella – Wiccans, Dianic, kitchen witchery, green witchery, hedge witchery, Alexandrian, eclectic, Faery, Gardnerian and Seax to name but a few. We at the Kitchen Witch Coven are very much based in kitchen/green/hedge witchcraft, although most of us have had training in Wicca, but we have also studied between us folk magic, hoodoo and druidry as well.

A lot of witches conform to a moral code called the Witches Rede (or the Wiccan Rede). It simply states: 'An it harm none, do what thou will.' This means that as long as you do no harm to anyone or anything, including yourself, you may do anything that your heart desires and has the willpower to accomplish. A witch who performs magic for the purposes of harm will ultimately be harming themselves. This comes about by the 'Threefold Law' that states that anything that you do will be returned to you three times. So if you perform good it will be returned to you threefold, likewise any evil will be returned to you threefold – so it makes sense to only do good. But, as with most things, this is your choice to make. You can decide to not follow a rede of any kind, but rely on your own moral code.

Witches practice magic, especially magic involving herbs, stones, colours, the elements and the energy of nature. However, we do not perform animal sacrifices; the only sacrifices made are of a spiritual nature.

Magic is the use of a witch's will and energy to manipulate and alter the probability of things around them. The only tool necessary to create magic is a strong will and focused intention. However, many witches will use a variety of tools as they feel the need for them to create their desired effect. Magic works in accordance with natural law and will not create unlikely affects, such as fireballs, bolts of lightning, or resurrect the dead. Well, not that I know of, anyway.

In my little dream world that I sometimes frequent I would have a big old farmhouse in the country with a huge kitchen that housed an old oak kitchen table big enough for everyone to sit around and have cups of tea and chat, herbs hanging to dry from the ceiling, a back garden big enough to host rituals and a view across the fields. In reality I live in a beautiful but modest 1920s terraced house on the outskirts of a city. I do have a garden and

I do have a large oak table, although it is in the dining room rather than the kitchen, but it is where everyone ends up sitting with cups of tea and slices of cake… there has to be cake to chat. I have lots of pots of herbs in my small garden and I have them hanging to dry in the conservatory so I don't do too badly. I have lived in a farmhouse in the middle of a field and in reality it is cold in the winter, muddy and desperately inconvenient if you run out of teabags…

I am lucky that within a short driving distance I have group rituals available to me, my own Kitchen Witch Coven has Sabbat rituals in a beautiful forestry setting, the Dorset Grove I belong to have their rituals in an ancient henge by a Saxon church and we also get to celebrate a couple of times a year within Stonehenge so I do consider myself lucky.

But, having said all that, you don't need beautiful ancient settings to have wonderful rituals, you can do a perfectly good ritual in your own front room – a kitchen witch's mottos are 'make the most of what you have' and 'adapt what you have to suit'.

I have always thought that sacred places are beautiful, but not always sacred to everyone. Some places I have visited that others have raved about have done nothing for me. Everyone is individual and we all have different favourite spots and different places that feel special to us. One of my very favourite sacred places is my own home. It is a place where I feel loved and a place that I feel safe in. It also has everything I need to hand and always has a good supply of cold chocolate in the fridge.

Chapter 2

Sacred Space

I guess the subject of sacred places leads me on to talking about sacred space. What is it and do you need it? Well, it is up to you, whether you are 'out of the broom closet', whether you actually have the physical space for it and whether the rest of your household mind you having besoms on the wall and cauldrons on the dinner table or not.

Sacred space can be created in your head and it is actually a good meditation tool to have a specific 'landscape' created in your mind that you can escape to when you need to. At least if the space is in your head you can decorate it any way you like; space and budget are not considerations.

Then you could have just a shelf with bits and pieces on it, or a cupboard that holds all your witchy paraphernalia.

If you have a spare bedroom that no one minds you using, it would be ideal to set up as a meditation/sacred room.

I don't have a spare bedroom, well not yet; it will be a few years before one of the children leaves home! But I do have the luxury of a very patient and understanding family who are quite used to having a broomstick hanging on the kitchen wall and statues of 'naked reindeer man' as my youngest calls my statue of Cernunnos on the mantelpiece.

It is as with all things about striking a balance that everyone within your household can live with.

Chapter 3

My Kitchen

Step into my kitchen for a while…

As a kitchen witch I work with what I have to hand, as you will see in the Magical Tools chapter where I give everyday options. The same goes for anything within the Craft. I have given in this book a broad overview of how I work with witchcraft along with the basics of Wiccan/more formal witchcraft structure, but go with the flow and work with what you feel is right for you.

So, back to my kitchen. This is where I spend a lot of time; I love to cook and I love making up medicine bags, witches bottles and the like (see further chapters), so the kitchen is the heart of my home. My kitchen probably doesn't look like most kitchens. Oh, it has the basic worktops, cupboards, fridge/freezer and cooker, but it also has a broomstick hanging on one wall, Hallowe'en signs on the walls and flying witches and witches balls suspended from the ceiling (yes I have a very tolerant husband!) along with shelves full of jars of herbs, all marked up with their magical properties.

Now your kitchen doesn't have to look like mine, but it works for me, stepping into it makes me feel at home, it puts me in the right frame of mind to work and to create, whether it is for a spell or to make the family dinner.

I don't want you all worrying that I cook up eye of newt and wing of bat (which incidentally were real folk names for herbs originally) for the family meal, really I don't! But I do like to add a bit of magic to my cooking.

I have an altar in my kitchen, just a small one; it is a lovely Green Man shelf. Before I start to cook I give a blessing to the altar, asking deity to watch over me whilst I cook and to add energy to the ingredients.

Each and every ingredient that is used in any meal has an energy of its own and a magical property. Cinnamon, for instance, is an excellent ingredient as it not only adds love and passion; it is also good for prosperity and protection.

Adding a pinch of herbs to your cooking can add the magical properties that come with it. Popping a bit of basil into a salad adds courage and strength, mint brings success and protection and rosemary dispels negative energy.

When you are stirring the saucepan or casserole dish, the wooden spoon becomes your wand and the stirring deosil (clockwise) becomes your way of adding positive energy to the food.

And don't forget the appliances too. The freezer and the fridge are good for working spells – if you need to 'freeze' some thoughts or emotions or 'cool off' a relationship, write it on a slip of paper and pop it in the freezer or the fridge until the spell is done.

Chapter 4

Energy

I think one of the first things that anyone needs to learn about if they are starting to walk the path of a witch is to learn how to work with energy.

Energy is used when we send healing, when we cast a spell, when we are in ritual and when we charge candles and herbs with intent.

Every living thing has its own energy, whether it is a flower, a crystal, a person or a pebble. All of the ingredients you might gather together for a spell will have their own individual energies and characteristics. If you use a wand, that has its own energy too, but the real energy comes from YOU.

Working with energy is really a combination. You can draw energy up from the Earth or from an item such as a crystal and you channel it through yourself, but you also add a bit of energy from your inner self as you do so. When you are in ritual you might also call upon the God and Goddess to lend their energy to your workings and you can raise energy from other sources as well. The elements can provide us with energy too – earth, air, fire and water all provide sources of energy that we can tap into.

But generally you are also the conduit, you summon the energy, you gather it, you add to it and you direct it.

Everyone has energy within them, everyone has the power to access it, to tap into it and use it. Unfortunately most people have no idea how to do so, and boy are they missing out!

The energy created by our bodies and by the spirit within our bodies is generally referred to as the aura. The energy that flows around and through our bodies is usually referred to as chi.

Part of being a witch is to be connected to the Earth, her plants and her creatures; to be aware of the energies around us so that we can connect and interact with them.

My favourite way of explaining energy is to ask people to rub their hands together briskly for a few seconds, then slowly pull them apart – you should be able to 'feel' the energy between them. Sometimes it takes a bit of practice, but when you do feel it – this is the energy you need to be working with. Once you can feel the energy, try to make it into energy 'balls', stretch it, squash it, experiment with it! (No throwing energy balls at people though, because that's not nice…)

Energy can be raised in many ways, it can be drawn up from the Earth, it can be taken from the universe, and it can be raised by drumming, singing, chanting or dancing.

The energy can then be directed. This can be done by sending it to the person you are healing, sending it out to the universe to be used where necessary, or when in ritual it is usually shaped into a cone of power. In a cone of power the energy is raised by those present and forms a spiralling cone in the centre of the circle to be released by the High Priestess and directed to its target.

On a smaller scale we raise and direct energy when we work a spell, for instance a candle spell. We would take the energy from the Earth, channel it through our body and out through our hands and into a candle, this will charge the candle with energy. We add our intent and any other 'ingredients' such as herbs and oils. Once the candle is burning it releases the energy we filled it with, that energy then goes on its merry way to fulfil the intent that it was meant for.

Chapter 5

Our Minds

How many minds do you have? There is the old saying, 'I am in two minds', but in actual fact we have three. Understanding how our three minds work helps us to work with magic.

Your conscious mind, your middle self

The first mind I want to talk about is the conscious mind, the one we are probably most familiar with. This is where you will find your personality and your ego. This is the mind that deals with everyday life when we are awake.

The conscious mind houses our reason, our logic, and our ability to analyse and stay alert. It deals with life as a series of events in a timeline, one after another. It sees life as sorted into compartments – past, present and future. The conscious mind is actually pretty good at remembering past events, dealing with the present and working out what it wants for the future, all at the same time.

It is your conscious mind that works out what you want for yourself and for your magic. It is limited though in that it does see things as linear, which doesn't allow us to work through large amounts of energy or information.

The psychic mind, your lower self, your younger self

The second mind I want to talk about is the psychic mind. This is where you will find the key to your magical abilities. It has no limitations. It works with intuition. Intuition leads us into our psychic abilities. Have you ever known who was at the door before you opened it, or known who was on the telephone before answering it? That is your psychic mind at work.

This mind is called the lower self because it comes from our unconscious and our subconscious. As we relax our logical conscious mind we move into our subconscious, which allows us to see things with greater insight.

Much as it might be a nice idea to always live in the subconscious, we need the balance of the conscious mind and the psychic mind to be able to function properly.

The minds work together in harmony.

The divine mind, the higher self, the older self

The psychic mind works as a connection between the conscious mind and the divine mind, which is the third mind or the higher self.

The divine mind is our spirit; it is what connects us to the whole. You can call this mind the Goddess, the God, the Divine Spirit. This level is a super consciousness, a higher self, an older self. It can see things from a higher perspective spiritually and mentally. It is not bound by linear time or logic. It is aware of all things, on all levels, at all times. The divine self knows what the conscious mind can handle so it drip feeds information so as not to overwhelm it.

It is the divine self that controls our dreams and intuition; it uses the psychic mind to relay this information. These symbols and messages are then deciphered by the unconscious and the subconscious.

The aim for any witch is to bring these three minds together so that they work as a team, so they are perfectly aligned. Once you have done this, magic will be so much easier.

A good little exercise to do each day is to visualise your three selves in harmony. This will have a positive effect on how you feel. Spend a couple of minutes each day to bring the lower self to the middle self, the middle self to the higher self and the higher self to the lower self so that they all harmonise together. When you get used to this exercise you will become aware of any harmony and any conflicts that your three selves have and you will know where the internal conflicts are.

States of consciousness

When you go into meditation or do any energy work you might notice that your state of consciousness changes. Moving into a different conscious state is one of the keys to working magic. To work the best magic, as I have said, we need our three minds to be in harmony with each other, so it helps to have a quick and easy method to bring the minds together. Eventually, with practice, this will become easier.

If you change your state of consciousness as a voluntary action then you won't lose yourself. You will still be able to concentrate, still work with energy and still have your intent in place.

This state of consciousness was called gnosis by the ancient Greeks; it means knowledge. It is in this state that you can get answers, solve problems, connect with deity and have a psychic connection.

When we go about our daily lives, working, eating, driving etc, our brainwaves are in a beta state. Once we move into meditation or working magic, if we have done it properly, our brainwaves move into an alpha state. It is a state of mind where we are relaxed but still aware of what is going on around us. Being in this alpha state (like you are when you are in a day dream) allows you to connect directly with your psychic mind. The next stage is theta brainwaves; this is the level you are at when you enter a deep trance, and the stage you enter when you are asleep. Then you have the delta state, which is the level your brainwaves are at when you are in a very deep sleep, a very deep trance or, indeed, a coma.

Chapter 6

Your Magical Name

Most, but not all, witches have a magical name – one that they use when they are in ritual, meditation or when working spells.

So how do you get one? Well, there are many ways. You could meditate and see if one is given to you. You could look through the internet and your books to see if anything jumps out at you. You could ask a friend or mentor to name you. Whatever way it happens, a magical name is very special. Some pagans don't like to share their magical name with others, choosing to keep it between themselves and the God or Goddess; after all a magical name carries power with it.

My own name came to me from various avenues. A while after I had found this path I visited a local Roman museum as they were holding a Celtic re-enactment day. There was lots going on, sword fights, dressing in Celtic outfits, making pottery, spinning and also several stalls showing how and what ancient Celts would have cooked. As I am a great lover of cooking and food it was to these stalls that I was drawn. It seemed to me that a lot of the recipes contained the herb tansy, the one that especially drew my eye was tansy cake. As I had already formed a connection with working with herbs I knew that Tansy was the right choice for a name, it fit and it has stayed with me. As for the Firedragon part of my name, that came from knowing that fire is my favourite element and that a love of dragons has been with me since I was a child. The names came to me and I meditated to check that they were right and the rest is history.

If you are looking for a magical name have a think about the following things:

Do you have a favourite name that you have liked for a very

long time or have always wished was your real name?

If you follow a particular tradition or path, what are some of the names of the God/desses associated with that tradition that you are drawn to, honour, or enjoy speaking with?

What are your favourite colours and what do those colours make you think of?

What kind of plants do you like?

What kind of magical things do you like – faeries, mermaids, dragons?

Where are your favourite places to be in nature?

What is your favourite element (earth, air, fire, water)?

What is your favourite animal or creature?

What is your favourite season?

What is your favourite month?

For each of the four seasons (spring, summer, autumn, winter) what is your favourite plant, place to be, and animal?

What interests and hobbies do you have?

What areas of the Craft are your favourite? (Runes, candles etc)

What is your favourite place/country/town in the world?

Your answers to these questions may at least give you a short list with which to work from.

Chapter 7

Meditation

The image is of a new age hippy sitting cross legged chanting 'om' right? Well no, unless you want it to be! Meditation is such a useful tool – not only does it serve to calm us and to enable us to chill out at the end of the day, it can also set us up for the day ahead, it can be used to answer questions, to clarify situations, to connect with animal totems and to allow us to connect with deity, to make that connection with the divine.

If you can, just spare five minutes each day to meditate. It will be worthwhile.

I tend to meditate at the end of the day, just before I go to bed. I close my eyes and focus on my breathing. I then take myself off in my head to my sacred space, to meet the Cailleach, my animal totems or just to be peaceful and unwind.

The basics of good meditation are:

Making yourself comfortable

While twisting yourself into a pretzel shape might look spiritual, it probably won't be very comfortable, so either lie down or sit in a comfortable chair.

Finding a quiet place

You really do need some peace and quiet to meditate properly, so make sure you are somewhere you won't be disturbed by the phone or small children asking you to find their teddy.

Setting the scene

This is up to you and what you feel comfortable with. I like to have some incense burning to put me in the right frame of mind, but it is a personal choice.

Music or drumming

Occasionally I like to listen to some 'plinky plonky' music in the background, the Goddess Temple in Glastonbury always has some on very quietly and it does help send you off into the realms of meditation. Drumming works for me on occasion too, just the quiet, solid beat of a drum in the background. I have tried soundtracks of the ocean and that works very well too. But also no sound at all is very good.

Breathing

I find the best way for me to achieve a meditative state is to focus on my breathing, deep breaths in… deep breaths out, releasing any negative energy or thoughts on the outward breath and taking in healing and calming white light on the inward breaths. You can also count down – visualise a screen in your mind's eye and see numbers counting down on it, or visualise yourself stepping down ten steps or a staircase to reach a meditative state.

Guided meditations

I am OK at doing a meditation where I just let my mind take me where it wants to go, but I do really enjoy guided meditations. These are meditations that are recorded by others. They take you on specific journeys, it might be to cleanse your chakras, it might be to meet a Goddess or a totem animal, or it might just be a walk through a forest. I find them easy to follow, but I know others find them restrictive. My advice is to try both ways and see what suits you.

Chapter 8

Pathworking

Pathworking – sometimes called journeying, inner plane work or vision questing – is a form of meditation used a lot in shamanic practice. It is a structured meditation with a purpose to it, a guided journey into our inner world or onto other planes or other worlds, such as the Otherworld, or into the Land of Fae.

This type of journeying allows us to stretch ourselves, to dip into our inner power, to connect with divinity, to aid us in decision-making, to seek past lives and to connect with messengers and guides.

Pathworking allows us to go beyond our conscious mind and even our universe because it creates a link between our conscious and subconscious minds, allowing us to access memories and psychic skills we may not usually reach. It will also have lasting effects. Once you have pathworked and connected with those guides or powers it will become apparent in your everyday life.

When you have gained the skill to pathwork successfully you will be able to wander freely and safely within all the inner realms and connect with the divine to gain insight, to explore new ideas, to meet new guides and to expand your entire potential.

The basics of setting up a pathworking

Decide what you need from this trip. Why are you journeying? What path will you take? What is your destination? What or who would you like to encounter? Obviously you will probably encounter some things you didn't plan for, but that makes it even more worthwhile! What image do you want to use to take you from this world onto your journey? (i.e. a gate, a knothole in a tree, a doorway etc).

When you have decided upon those details you need a framework – starting with an induction, this is where you enter the pathworking, the trance-like state. Then decide on the body of the pathworking; this is whatever you need to do whilst on your journey, the reason you are doing it. Then decide the closure; how you leave the pathworking and come back to reality. The induction and the closure will be pretty close to your script, but the body may take different twists and turns other than those you expected.

It helps to write down your framework. I prefer to then record the pathworking to my phone or laptop so that I can listen to it, but go with what works for you.

The basic steps for pathworking are very similar to those for meditation:

1. Find a safe, quiet and comfortable place. Make sure you won't be disturbed.
2. Ground and centre.
3. Turn on your recording or just close your eyes to begin your journey. Visualise your induction point, the entry to your journey. Just listening to or visualising your induction should take you into your trance state, but if it doesn't, focus on your breathing to obtain a meditative state.
4. Visualise your induction, see yourself at the entry. Take a moment to fix that place in your mind. See yourself reaching out to touch the entryway, feel how real it is, notice all the details, the feel, any sounds, any smells.
5. Once you have the entry point in your mind solidly you can begin your journey.
6. Walking through the gateway, enter the body of your journey. Notice all the details – listen, touch, smell, hear, taste, take note of everything. Set the details in your mind so that you will recall them when you come back to reality. Sometimes even the smallest detail may be important.

7. If you meet anyone on your pathworking, whether it is a human, a deity, a fae, an animal, whatever, please be polite and respectful. Don't touch any animal or being without asking first. If you are asked to move on then do so with respect. These beings work on a different plane, you do not want to upset them. Do not take anything unless you know it has actually been given to you. Use your common sense and mind your manners!
8. When you have finished your pathworking, return to the point you started at. Go back to your gateway and go through it, but do so slowly, coming back to reality gently and calmly. And always ground afterwards (see the next chapter for details).

A traditional use of pathworking is to connect with the elements and the deities and elementals that work within those realms.

Chapter 9

Grounding and Centring

I want to talk a bit about grounding and centring.

This is important and not just when in ritual. You can ground and centre whenever you need to and in fact it is a useful trick to do during your day.

Grounding involves connecting with the Earth to calm and focus yourself. You know that totally hyper feeling you get sometimes? It might be after ritual, it might be when you have got yourself worked up into a complete hissy fit, and it might be because you have eaten too many marshmallows (ahem). Grounding allows you to drain off that excess energy and refocus. A simple grounding and centring exercise is:

Sit or stand still, clear your head as much as possible.
Visualise sending roots down from your legs, through your feet and into the earth.
Feel those roots reaching down through the soft, brown soil.
Visualise them searching down, down into the core of the very planet itself.

If you are really, seriously hyper, I find it helps to visualise your arms stretching up to the sky as well, feeling your arms, your hands and your fingers becoming branches and sprouting leaves.

Once your 'roots' have tapped into the Earth's core, feel the energy of that coming back up the roots, travelling right back up towards you. Feel it enter your centre, your very core being and feel it balance, focus and centre you.

That is grounding and centring, but you might find other ways that suit you better. Experiment and see what works for you.

Chapter 10

Shielding

A shield is a bubble of protective energy you can surround yourself with as a defence. It is essentially your aura, but you turn it into a protective shield that helps keep physical and mental harm from you.

It not only keeps you protected from negative energies that might be flying about, but it can also protect you from negative people. Do you ever find yourself completely drained of energy, really miserable or even physically ill after talking to someone? They probably aren't doing it on purpose, but negative people can literally suck the energy out of you if you don't have your personal shields up.

A protective shield

Make yourself comfortable and use your usual method of reaching a meditative state (focus on your breathing, counting down etc).

Become aware of your aura, the field of energy that surrounds your body. Visualise it as a bubble surrounding your whole body.

Visualise the outer skin of your bubble becoming a reflective surface. You can see out and send energy out, but nothing harmful can come back through. Hold the intent of protection in your mind.

If you wish, you can say some words of protection, something like: 'My personal shield is now charged to protect me from negative energies, may it keep me from harm and send positive energies back. So mote it be.' (OK, I am no poet, but you get the idea!)

Hold the image of your shield getting stronger until you feel safe enough. Then allow the image to dissipate. Come back out of your meditative state as you would usually.

Once you have this shield practised you can call upon it at any time, even if you are out shopping and it is busy and you feel vulnerable for example. Just visualise your aura forming into a protective, reflective shield.

I usually choose a reflective surface and am mindful that only negative energies cannot penetrate it, allowing positive energy to still come through. I would suggest not visualising a shield made up of something like bricks, because this would cut you off from all energies, and would make you too shut off. We do want to have some feelings!

You can put your shield in place before you go anywhere, but you can also bring it up in a split second if you feel threatened in anyway. I am a bit of a Star Trek fan so I also hear the voice of Commander Riker in my head saying, 'Shields up' – that is the key that sparks my shield into gear (yep, I can be a geek sometimes).

Chapter 11

Deity

Within the pagan world everyone will probably have a slightly different idea of deity; some think of it as Gods and Goddesses, some think of it as one Source and every other definition in between. It is somewhat a personal thing, and everyone will visualise the Gods and Goddesses in a very personal way. The God Thor may appear blond for one person and a red head to another.

Some might see 'traditional' deities – Gods and Goddess of various pantheons such as Athena, Woden, Aphrodite etc, or they may see deity as spirits in all things, the spirit of the forest, the spirit of the sea etc. Some may work with deity as energies such as Jack in the Green and the Moon Mother.

You will find your way as you grow on your own path; you may work with all sorts of deities, spirits and energies along the way until you become comfortable with what deity means for you, it will be an interesting journey!

Essentially, most witches work with the Goddess and probably, but not necessarily to a lesser extent, with the God. Female and masculine energies create a balance as a whole. Everything has energy; every living thing has an essence. Deity connects them all, bringing everything together. The Earth itself is a living thing. She is female energy and she is called by many names – Earth Goddess, Mother Earth, Gaia – she is the Maiden, the Mother, the Crone in all aspects, she is all seasons. Everything on our planet lies within Mother Earth, but all things are also separate.

Then we have the balance, we have the male energy, the Horned God, the Green Man. He is nature, he is the forest. He lives, he grows, he dies and he is reborn again. He is the consort of the Goddess.

When I first started on this path I was working through some lessons from a school that asked me to research different pantheons, so that is what I did. Actually it was a worthwhile exercise.

I settled upon the Celtic pantheon because it was the one I felt most comfortable with. I am from the UK so it seemed to be the most sensible route. Over the years I have worked with various deities from that pantheon. But I haven't worked with it exclusively; I have stepped outside and worked with Hawaiian deities, Greek and Roman deities and quite frequently Loas and Orishas. I prefer to work with a deity that suits my needs, one that feels right for the time, place and intent. And it's fun and interesting to explore a bit… you never know who you might meet!

I see deity as different facets of the One. For instance Athena, Pele, Brighid, Isis, the Morrigan are all Goddesses in their own right, each with their own unique energies, abilities and personalities, but I also see them as being part of the Goddess, each one a facet of a single diamond.

The Goddess is in all things, but in the main she has three major facets – the Triple Goddess. She is the Maiden, the Mother and the Crone. As the Maiden she is young, energetic, independent and carefree. She is fresh, representing new beginnings and creative ideas. As the Mother she is pregnant with potential and possibilities, she brings ideas into manifestation. Then she is the Crone, filled with wisdom, reflection and introspection. Our own lives follow this pattern, as the Moon does in her phases of waxing, full and waning.

The God, too, follows stages; he is energy, the rising sap, the death in autumn, the living forest. He forces growth and changes. He is the lord of the dance; he is fire, passion and energy, fertility and sexuality. He can be mischievous, but also protective and compassionate. He is both a son and a lover to the Goddess. He is the Holly King but also the Oak King, he is the Sky God and he is the Sun God and in these aspects he has many names in many cultures.

Working with deity is so immensely rewarding. We can call upon them to lend energy to our rituals, to our healing work, to spell work; we can ask them for guidance and assistance, for clarity, for comfort, to boost our confidence and to just be with us. But bear in mind when you ask for assistance it might not be exactly what you expected. Each deity is an individual and they all have their own very specific characters and personalities. You might have got yourself into a mess and ask a particular Goddess for some help and guidance, hoping for her to be kind and considerate, what you might get is a bit of butt kicking if she thinks that's what you deserve!

I would also add a caution here. I don't want to scare anyone, but just want to mention, please be polite, please be considerate, don't summon deity as if they were servants, they are higher beings and they can cause you a whole lot of trouble if you don't show respect. And if you have called upon them to help with something don't forget to thank them. It doesn't have to be a grand gesture; water some plants, feed the birds, put out an offering in the garden (something biodegradable) or if you have an altar set up, pop something on that as an offering, a crystal perhaps.

As I have said, each deity has its own personality and therefore each one has its own speciality if you like. They each deal with particular energies. So if you need some help with a healing spell you probably don't want to call a War God. Do some research and call upon the deity that fits the bill, if you are after some guidance in matters of the heart call upon help from a Goddess of Love, the results will be much better.

Sometimes we will work with a specific deity for just one meditation, call upon a particular deity for one spell or ritual, other times a deity will be with us for several months or even years. If you are really lucky you will at some point on your journey find a deity that becomes your patron deity, the one that you know is a perfect fit for you, and one that will always be with you no matter what. A patron deity will understand how you roll, they will know how your mind and heart work and will lend you support and strength, but be prepared because in my experience they will also tell you the truth and sometimes that's not easy to listen to! I had been in the Craft for nine years before I met my patron deity, the Cailleach, and she has been with me ever since. I was reading a fiction book, a story about witches (of course). The Cailleach Bheur was one of the characters and I immediately felt drawn to her. Then I kept seeing her name mentioned in other places – on the internet and in other nonfiction books I was reading. I did a bit of research about her and it all made so much sense. So I sat down one evening and meditated specifically to meet with her and ask, which is what I did; I asked her if she was my patron Goddess and got a resounding 'Yes'. She is strong and feisty and doesn't mince her words, but she is also caring and supportive. She will poke me if I need prompting and she will tell me in no uncertain words if she thinks I have been a plum. She is, however, a Winter Goddess so during the summer months, although she is still with me, she fades slightly. In the past couple of years she has taken to giving me another Goddess to work with for the warmer months. Last year it was Aine, this year it was the Lady of Avalon, and I have learnt a lot and enjoyed the experience.

Meditation to meet a deity

Make yourself comfortable; make sure you won't be disturbed. Close your eyes and focus on your breathing.

Visualise yourself in a clearing in forest. The grass under your feet is lush and green; the trees around you are tall and swaying slightly in the breeze, the leaves rustling as the air winds around them. You see a pathway that leads you from the clearing between a gap in the trees so you follow it. While you walk take in the scents around you, the sounds of the leaves rustling, the wildlife snuffling in the undergrowth and the birds singing in the tree tops.

As you pass through the gap in the trees you find yourself in between sand dunes that lead down to the shoreline of a large and beautiful ocean.

You follow the path down through the dunes, feeling the sand under your feet.

When you reach the edge of the water you stop and look around you to take in your surroundings. You can hear the crash of the waves on the shore as you stand and slowly turn in a circle.

To your right are mountain tops, some of them so high that the tips are covered in snow. Behind you is the forest that you came from and to your left it looks like the ocean narrows into an inlet of a river.

So many different landscapes – the roaring, crashing ocean that glints in the sunlight, the cool mountain ranges that take over the skyline and the cool, fresh green forest.

Sit yourself down on the sand and ask if there is a deity present who would like to come to meet with you.

A figure appears from one of the directions. They walk towards you. What do they look like? What are they wearing? What impressions do you get from them as they approach you?

When you meet, give a greeting. Ask if they have any messages for you, if they are here to work with you or if they have any advice to give you. Ask whatever questions come to mind, but always be respectful.

Sit a while and talk with them.

When you are ready, thank them for their time and bid them farewell.

Make your way back up through the sand dunes, following the path back through the gap in the trees and into the clearing in the forest.

Slowly the forest clearing dissipates and you are back in your own reality.

Wriggle your fingers and toes, stretch your arms and open your eyes.

Chapter 12

Tools

There are a recognised set of tools that are used in witchcraft, but as a kitchen witch myself I tend to be fairly flexible on these. As a newcomer to the Craft I thought I had to rush out and purchase all these things because I needed all the right tools to get the job done… you don't. Something that comes with experience, something that you learn over time, is that really you don't need a fancy sparkly athame, although it might look pretty. A kitchen knife does the same job. I'm not saying don't buy all these things, but I am saying you don't NEED to buy them, especially if you are working to a budget. Be inventive, create your own tools, make them from natural items or look through charity shops/thrift stores and buy things second hand.

Here's a list of magical tools, in alphabetical order:

Altar cloth

I love to change the cloth on my altars (yep I have more than one altar) to suit the seasons, but you don't have to. Some of my altar cloths were purchased from occult stores with the sole purpose of decorating my altar, some are old scarves that I had, and some are just a yard or two of satin and chiffon that I purchased on eBay. Get creative, go with your flow and see where it takes you. I have some wicked red and black spiderweb fabric I use at Samhain (purchased on eBay) and I have some lovely bright coloured satin that I overlay with different colour chiffon to create a lovely effect. Red satin with gold chiffon overlay is perfect for the Autumn Equinox, for instance. But you can get some beautiful large scarves cheaply in discount stores and charity shops; you might even find a few in the back of granny's closet if you ask nicely!

Asperger

It took me some time before I realised what this was. You don't seem to hear the word very often, but it is actually the official name for the small brush that is used in ritual to sprinkle blessed water. Sometimes it is made from twigs, sometimes from feathers or even dried lavender stems tied together – easy to make if you want to use one. In our rituals we tend to dip our fingers in the water and flick… it is way more fun ;-)

Athame (pronounced ah-tha-may)

This is essentially a dagger. It is ceremonial, usually not sharp and represents the masculine. It is often used in ceremonial magic rituals placed into a chalice to represent the male and female union. (Come on think about it…) It is also used for directing energy and casting circles. You can get some absolutely beautiful athames; I have one myself that was gifted to me that has the Triple Goddesses around the handle. I also have a very plain, simple athame with a natural wooden handle and a brass blade. You can purchase a pretty athame, you could also make one out of wood if you are handy or you can also just adapt a kitchen knife. I have had my small athame for many years and only ever used it once to cast a circle… the rest of the time it sits on my altar collecting dust.

Bell

Again this is something that I just had to have at the beginning and really haven't used it much at all. That's not saying you won't though. A bell is good to use when you need a quick fix to dispel negative energy in the house. Ring the bell in each room to clear the air. It can be used to call quarters in ritual and can also be useful to help induce trance and meditation.

Besom/broomstick

You've got to have one of these for when you need to nip down the shops in a hurry ;-) The besom is used before a ritual to sweep away negative energies, it is only symbolic as the broom bristles never actually touch the floor (otherwise the besom would just get full up with dust and rubbish). You can also use a besom to symbolically sweep through your house if it needs a good shake up, to shoot any negativity out of the door. I also have a small besom hanging in my porch, bristles up – this helps keep unwanted guests away. The besom is also used in handfastings, the couple jump over it to signify their pledge. There are some beautiful handmade besoms available. Keep an eye out at local country fairs. Also keep an eye out in the shops during Hallowe'en. Quite often they have some really pretty, natural besoms to go with costumes that can be utilised.

Boline

Now this is the fancy name for the knife used to cut herbs. It usually has a white handle and will usually have a curved blade. It can also be utilised for carving symbols on candles for spell work. I have to admit I don't own one. When I need to cut herbs I use secateurs, when I need to carve candles I use a large pin, but if you fancy owning one go for it.

Cake

Yep you read it right. During most rituals some sort of bread or cake will be shared. In my coven and in my grove it is always cake, why? Because it's nice (and because the Grove Arch Druid happens to be a baker). It is also good to eat something after a ritual or any energy work as it helps to ground you. Chocolate works well too (that's my excuse and I am sticking to it).

Candles

Oh how I love candles! They can be used as representations of the God and Goddess on your altar, as symbols of the elements, as the element of fire, and used in spell work, meditation and divination.

Cauldron

Every witch has to have one of these surely? Would you be a witch without one? Yes, you do really need something cauldronish, but it doesn't have to be a fancy iron one. It can just be an old casserole dish. The cauldron is a symbol of feminine; it represents a womb and also corresponds to the element of water. I use my cauldron for burning things – incense, herbs, spells etc so really all you need is a pot-shaped vessel that is fire proof.

Censer

This is a little pot on a chain for burning incense in (visualise a Roman Catholic priest swinging a brass pot around church wafting smoke). It is useful in ritual if you have to walk around the circle with it, but you could also use a small cauldron, brazier or fire-proof pot.

Chalice

This is a cup or goblet. It holds water or wine and represents the feminine. I have a very pretty silver one that I purchased in my mad rush to collect all the 'essentials' when I first started. I think I used it once and now it sits in the cupboard. But, we do use a very pretty glass one at our rituals that is passed around for everyone to take a sip of the wine or mead (usually only fruit juice) contained therein. I do also own a lovely gothic chalice with a dragon curled around, but that I use on my dragon altar and have never used it to actually drink from, it's just pretty! You can buy a dramatic or pretty chalice, you could also use a pretty wine glass, tumbler or any kind of drinking vessel. Have a look in the supermarkets or charity stores.

Cords

These are used in various areas of the Craft; for knot magic, to mark boundaries and in initiations.

Crystals and stones

Surely every self respecting witch owns a crystal or two? They are one of those things that once you have one you will usually start a whole collection and it doesn't stop. Crystals are useful for so many things; they all have their own unique energies and qualities. They can be used in spell work, ritual, meditation, healing and offerings. Stones and crystals can range from a simple beach pebble right up to a diamond and all the other semi-precious gems in between.

Crystal ball

The traditional fortune teller's refrain is: 'Just cross my palm with silver.' Not everyone will want or use a crystal ball, some of the larger ones are incredibly expensive, but I have a couple of small ones that fit in the palm of my hand, they are beautiful and work very well for divination.

Drum

Useful but not essential. Used in ritual to raise energy, I also use mine in meditation and trance work. It doesn't have to be fancy, although there are some beautiful bohdrans out there. If you don't want to spend lots of money, make one. All you need is an old biscuit or sweet tin. I actually learnt to the play the drums using a plastic tub with a lid on.

Incense

This can be a loose mixture burnt on charcoal, or can be cones or sticks. Incense is used to clear negative energy, create sacred space, complement spell work or add energy to a ritual. If you can't use incense for health reasons try using essential oil on a burner or scented candles.

Mortar and pestle

I have a very pretty stone mortar and pestle that I keep in my work room purely for magical use. Not for magical reasons but because I sometimes use it to grind up items that might be poisonous to ingest such as mistletoe berries – it would be a bit disastrous to then use it to make a nice spice mix to go on chicken for dinner. If you don't have a mortar and pestle, use the end of a rolling pin in a small pot.

Offering dish/libation bowl

I have several offering dishes on my altars. One is Goddess shaped and purchased in Glastonbury, two I made myself from air drying clay, one is a large shell I found on the beach and one is a glass dish I purchased for a few pence in a charity shop. I also have one in the garden which is just a large flat stone I collected from Tintagel. These little bowls are used to leave offerings to the Gods, spirits or the fae. Pretty much anything can be left as an offering, go with what feels right for you and what you think the particular deity or fae might like. I usually put a couple of crystals in my Goddess offering dish. I leave honey and milk outside for the fae, whilst a lot of the Orisha spirits like rum and tobacco.

Sword

I have used a sword in ritual to cast a circle. They are usually mighty heavy and a bit unwieldy, but if you like the King Arthur thing go with it!

Staff

I have a very beautiful staff that was gifted to me. They aren't essential, but can be used to cast circles and direct energy, and are also representative of the God. They seem to be used a lot more by druids than witches. There are many beautiful staffs, some of them very ornate, but you can make your own. Just take a walk in your local woods and find a fallen branch that is the right height and shape. Clean it up and voila! A staff is born. If you feel the urge you could carve symbols on it, tie ribbons or feathers around it or even stick crystals on the top.

Wand

You've got to have a wand... One of those silver sparkly ones with glitter? Well yes, if that's what takes your fancy, have one. You can make a wand out of a piece of wood, sand it or leave it natural, carve runes or symbols onto it, tie ribbons and feathers to it – make it your own. The added bonus of having a wooden wand is that you can use the energies from the tree the wood came from. You could have wands made from different types of trees to use in different rituals or for different spells. Alternatively, you could use a wooden spoon from your kitchen or just your finger!

Chapter 13

Altars

As I have mentioned my altars a few times already guess I better talk about them properly.

What is an altar?

I looked up the word in the dictionary just out of interest and this is the description it gives:

> *An elevated place or structure, as a mound or platform, at which religious rites are performed or on which sacrifices are offered to gods, ancestors etc.*

When I had finished laughing, I thought about it – this is the description of what ancient altars were. It seems that it needs a bit of tweaking to represent modern day altars, otherwise there are going to be some very worried sacrificial goats out there!

An altar to me is a small place, an area that is set aside where you can place items in honour of deity, leave offerings, sit and meditate, a place to connect with deity and a place to leave spells to 'do their thing'. It isn't just a pretty place to keep your magical goodies, although that is part of it, for me an altar is also a place to honour deity. Over time and with use your altar will become a sacred place and it will gather magical energy from the workings, meditations and items that you have used it for or placed on it.

You don't have to have a huge ornate table with dragons carved up the legs and gold inlay on the top, an altar can just be a small space on your mantelpiece or bookshelf, it can be the top of a coffee table. If you are still 'in the broom closet' or sharing your space with others you could keep your altar on a tray and just slide it into a cupboard. If you don't have anywhere inside the house to use you could always just set aside a small space in the garden, just a clear patch of earth that you can leave stones, flowers and shells on.

I have several altars, but then I have a very understanding family. I have a small altar in the kitchen, it is actually a Green Man face with a shelf on top of his head, and the shelf space is only the size of my hand. On it I keep a small vase, which was actually a glass taper candlestick holder, just big enough for one flower from my garden. I also have a very tiny feather, pebble, red crystal and shell on it to represent the four elements. It is my kitchen witch altar and one that I give thanks and blessings to when I am working in the kitchen.

I also have an altar in my living room, a lovely low wooden table that was gifted to me. This altar is for the Orisha Oshun and the Loa Papa Legba whom I work with a lot. On it is a beautiful statue of Oshun that I purchased for a few euros in a French supermarket of all places. I have a wooden pentacle standing next to it, a shell for offerings, a small pot for flowers (an upturned lid of a bottle) and a veve, which is a symbolic drawing calling upon the spirit of Papa Legba. I also keep lots of candles and crystals on this altar too.

Then there is my working altar (seriously my family are wonderfully patient with me). This sits on top of a small chest of drawers in the dining room. This is the room that I spend a lot of my time in, it is where I write, where I put together my crafts and where I plot and scheme. Usually this altar has an image of whatever deity I am working with at the time (at the moment it has a picture of the Lady of Avalon above it) and I decorate it with the seasons. As I write this, it is heading to Mabon, so I have a red satin cloth with a gold chiffon cloth over the top. It has a large gold candle, a red candle holder, a red Goddess representation, my Goddess offering dish, my dragon candle holder and is covered with nuts, berries, blackberries and apples (all pretend ones). It also has my friendship candle – a small glass candle holder with a blue candle inside and crystals around it to represent my sisters in the Craft. A scroll sits beside it with our dedication to each other on. This is the altar I use for any spells or workings and to connect with deity.

And then… my main altar, which is situated on the bottom shelf of my bookshelves. The shelves themselves are filled with all my favourite witchy books. This altar is more fixed in that I change the altar cloth for the seasons, but the items on it stay pretty much the same. There are candles to represent deity, my figure of Granny Weatherwax from the Terry Pratchett books (the ultimate representation of what a strong, powerful witch should look like in my opinion), a statue of Merlin, a representation of my main totem Boar, my athames, my crystal ball, offering dishes and crystals. At Samhain this is the altar that also holds my honour to the ancestors – photos of my grandparents and great grandparents who have passed over, together with an assortment of their jewellery.

My conservatory houses my work desk and all my herbs, spices, crystals and ingredients for making witches bottles, poppets, medicine bags and the like. On the top of the desk is another small altar, it is a small oak slab and on this I have a magpie wing, a magpie skull (another of my totems) and magpie feet – all I hasten to add taken from road kill, a yew wand and two very large rusty nails.

And lastly (I hear you give a sigh of relief) I have an outside altar, a large stone from Tintagel that is my altar to the Cailleach who is my patron Goddess. This altar is very simple, it has a couple of hag stones on, occasionally a feather and that is about it.

I have seen all sorts of altars ranging from a pile of stones to huge grand affairs dripping in gold and splendour. Ultimately your altar is a reflection of you and should be so. Be creative and go with what you feel is right and what suits you.

Altars can be used for many intents; you may just want to

have a main one or a working one. You might also like to set up an altar specifically for healing or one with the intent of prosperity. The options are really limitless.

There are traditional items and positions involved in creating an altar and I will share my interpretation of them here, but I can't stress enough how important I feel it is to go with what feels right for you as an individual. If you want an altar with fluffy toys, sparkly tiaras and offerings of chocolate sweets on it – go for it!

How you set up your altar is really up to you and what feels right, but traditionally the Goddess items are placed on the left and the God items on the right. The altar is a reflection of a ritual circle, so if you use representations of the elements then they should technically be placed to correspond with the right directions too.

If you belong to a particular tradition or coven they may have strict rules about these things. If you are unsure, ask. They may have underlying concepts of why they do things a particular way. However, I don't believe the traditional rules are hard and fast. Nothing is WRONG. If you think an item feels right in a particular place then go with it. I am a firm believer of the 'if it feels right for you, do it' school of thought.

I would mention that if you have pets such as cats be careful what offerings and items you leave on your altar as things such as chocolate are not good for cats that like to 'invade' altars!

Chapter 14

Cleansing and Consecrating

We cleanse and consecrate our magical tools, crystals and divination tools and I have even done it to pieces of jewellery.

We cleanse to clear away any negative energy. All items pick up energies if they have had previous owners, from the store keepers, from the air around them. Some of the energies might be good, some might be a bit icky, so it is a worthwhile process to cleanse any new piece of kit that you purchase or are gifted.

We consecrate the same items to imbue them with our own energies. Especially in the case of magical tools or divination tools, we need them to recognise us and our unique energy so that they will work in tandem with our spirit.

For instance, if you purchase a pack of tarot cards and someone else has been playing with them, they will have picked up the energies from that person. If you then use them to do a reading for yourself without cleansing and consecrating them the reading may be a bit squiffy for you because it may be confused with the energy still hanging about from the other person.

There are several ways of cleansing an item. How you choose to do it will vary depending on what you have to hand, what the item is, how patient you are and how you roll personally.

Visualisation

The easiest way to cleanse and the one that requires no props is to visualise. Hold the item in your hand or hold your hands over the item and visualise a cleansing bright white light coming from spirit/the universe/the Earth through you, down your arm and out of your hands into the object. The white light will flush out any negative energy.

Sun and the Moon

You could use the energy from the Sun or the Moon to cleanse and charge your items, this works especially well with crystals. Leave the item out in the sunlight or in the moonlight to be cleansed and charged with pure energy.

Breath

Another easy one is to use the power of breath. Ground and centre yourself, focus on the item and then very gently breathe on it, visualising your breath as being cleansing and purifying.

Incense

Incense is used a lot to cleanse, whether it is by passing the item through the smoke of the incense itself or by using incense to smudge something – your home, your body or an item. The power of the smoke cleanses and purifies.

Nature

As long as you have a safe place and the item won't be damaged you can leave it outside for the weather to do the job. Wind is an excellent element to cleanse an item.

Burying

Burying your item under the soil is another good idea, but make sure that the item won't be damaged, especially if the soil is very wet, and please remember where you buried it! The soil acts with the power and energy of the Earth to cleanse the item. I used this method to clean the magpie skull I had.

Water

Good for crystals, as long as they aren't porous. Run items under a tap or, if you can, in the running water of a stream or the ocean. Just make sure to hang on to them!

Flame

Passing an item through or just over the flame of a candle also works well. Be careful not to burn yourself or the item. Use your visualisation skills with this one, imagine the flame growing and surrounding the item, burning off all the negative energies.

To consecrate

Once the item has been cleansed you can consecrate it. Use your visualisation powers and send a bright white light into the item and ask that the God and Goddess bless it and consecrate it for your use. If you feel poetically inclined you could also write a blessing chant to go with it.

Chapter 15

The Moon

The Moon and her phases play an important part in the life of a witch. She is the Goddess in her many forms whether she is the Waxing Moon of the Maiden Goddess, the Full Moon of the Mother Goddess, the Waning Moon of the Crone Goddess or the Dark Moon of the Dark Goddess.

The phases of the Moon have great meanings and impacts on us and the planet we live on. The Moon commands the tides of the oceans, for a start.

I am not going to go into the scientific details of the Moon and her phases here; I am going to focus on the magical details, because that's what I work with, a scientist I am not.

Each phase of the Moon carries with it particular qualities that we can utilise when doing our spell working. The phase of the Moon adds power to our spells. You will probably also find that it will affect your mood and happenings around you too.

New Moon

This is a wonderful time to make new beginnings of all types. It is especially good for getting rid of bad habits. Habitual ways of thinking that are harmful and negative can also be abandoned at this time. It is also a good time to start something creative. New projects at work can also be launched.

The first day of the New Moon is really best devoted to the planning stages of ventures. It is good to feel just a little excited and filled with anticipation, although your energy may not be at its highest. A day or two into the cycle is the time to take the initiative, apply for that job and start house hunting or any similar endeavours. It is good for beauty, health, self-improvement, farms and gardens, job hunting, love and romance, and networking. It offers protection and creates a shield for the beginning of the cycle.

Crescent Moon magic

Crescent Moon magic is worked as the Moon rises at mid-morning and sets after sunset. It is good for animals, business, change, emotions and matriarchal strength. It represents the zest of life with the aid of stability and helps bring forth courage and optimism.

Waxlng Moon

Now your projects can get into their stride. Be aware, however, that overstrains are more likely at this time and that the body takes things in and absorbs them more readily with a Waxing Moon.

It is a good time to build yourself up if you have been unwell or tired. Absorbing, boosting your energy and taking in supplies are crucial now. Go on an active holiday, get in touch with friends, plan a party, arrange meetings, and increase communication.

As Full Moon approaches notice what isn't working and shed it in order to focus your energies more effectively. Remind yourself to slow down a little and conserve your strength.

It is good for courage, elemental magic, friends, luck and motivation. It gives vitality, courage and strength and stimulates the heart. This is also a good time to review work already in progress and to gain insights.

Gibbous Moon magic

The power of the Gibbous Moon is good for patience, purity and protection. It creates the right atmosphere for meditation and centring. It represents innocence.

Full Moon

Hold a party or an event, but be aware that the energy level is likely to be high and anything troublesome is likely to surface. Cook and stock up the freezer. Pay special attention to your creative ventures and your dreams.

This is a good time to try out forms of divinations such as scrying or tarot. Reflect about your goals, feelings and matters that have to do with relationship and family.

As the Full Moon just passes, the time arrives to put the finishing touches on what you have been doing and to get ready for the quieter time to come. Enjoy beauty and art, listen to music. If you have argued with someone, but do not feel the issues are really vital, make up now.

Just after the Full Moon is a good time for artistic endeavours, beauty, health, fitness, change and decisions. Things associated with this time include children, competition, dreams, families, health and healing, knowledge, legal undertakings, love and romance, money, motivation, protection, psychism and self-improvement. The light starts to enlighten inner wisdom. It provides clarity, alertness and optimism and also aligns the right use of will.

Light a pink candle dressed with rose oil and burn it to bring romance and good friendships. Dress a green candles with patchouli oil, charge it with the intent of prosperity, and burn the candle every night for two weeks. Bake fresh basil leaves into cheese bread or scone mix then cut the bread into circles. Eat them for prosperity. To bring success charge a piece of citrine in the Full Moon light and carry in your purse for a month.

Disseminating Moon magic

This is good for addictions, decisions, divorce, emotions, stress, and protection. It builds knowledge, sharing, calming, vocal expression and communication. It aids in meditation and enhances inner attunement.

Waning Moon/last quarter

You do not have to be concerned so much about overdoing things now because the lunar rhythm will act as something of a brake. Now is a good time to throw away your rubbish, take old clothes to charity shops. Consider how well things are working out and analyse information. Follow your needs and reactions.

It is good for addictions, divorce, health and healing, banishing disease, and protection from stress. There is a transformation from negative vibrations to positive. This balances the energy within the body and helps the mind and body flow more easily with life. This is a good time for rest and contemplation. Review your magical work and gain insight into what needs to be eliminated as the Moon moves towards the dark. It is a good time to review your diet and your health in general. Sort through any relationship problems or issues at this phase of the Moon. It is also a good time to do a ritual or meditation to restore balance in your life.

Dark Moon/balsamic magic

This is good for tackling addictions, change, divorce, enemies, justice, obstacles, quarrels, removal, separation, stopping stalkers and theft. It is also a suitable time for working on universal love of self and others. It draws love to you and removes sorrows and past hurts. The Moon at this phase is calming, protective, and serene. It improves relationships. It is a good time for divination. When the last quarter of the Moon has disappeared, write the name of something you wish to decrease on to the side of a black candle and burn it every night until the New Moon. (Be careful here, remember to state 'and it harm none'.) Leave your altar bare of flowers at this time. Burn only dark coloured candles or none at all. Use sombre incense such as myrrh and patchouli. Raise energy with slow drumming or chanting or keep your rites low key. Call on the wisdom of the Crone Goddesses. Use this time to eliminate or banish bad habits.

You may feel more like meditating and being alone. Clear spaces of all descriptions and make endings. Some people favour scrying and meditation with the Dark Moon because it is a more inward time. The insights you glean now will have a deeper, more insightful quality, whereas at Full Moon they may be more obviously creative.

Blue Moon

Most years have twelve full moons that occur approximately monthly. In addition to those twelve full lunar cycles, each solar calendar year contains roughly 11 days more than the lunar year of 12 lunations (one lunar phase cycle). The extra days accumulate, so every two or three years there is an extra full moon and we call that a 'Blue Moon'. A true Blue Moon occurs when there are four full moons in a single season. The definition of a Blue Moon being the second full moon in a single month was first brought into play in 1946 by a writer who had an article in a Maine farmers guide who had decided that a Blue Moon should be the second full moon in a month and, effectively, changed a long held definition of a Blue Moon being a seasonal thing, not a monthly thing

The saying 'once in a blue moon' doesn't mean never it just means on a rare occasion.

I don't know of any particularly specific magic that should be worked on a Blue Moon, I would just treat it as an extra bonus Full Moon! Although the Blue Moon is also known as the Goal Moon so it would be an excellent time to set new goals for yourself.

As it is also something that only occurs on occasion, I would treat it as a good time to ask for those very special 'once in a Blue Moon' requests, something really special – the once in a lifetime kind of wish.

Use the Full Moon for any immediate need: a sudden boost of power or courage; a change of career; location or travel; psychic protection; healing acute medical conditions; a large sum of money needed urgently; consummation of love or making a permanent love commitment; justice; ambition and promotion.

Planning spells

Before performing spells and rites, it is a good idea to meditate about what one is trying to achieve and how. The phase of the Moon is something on which to reflect. Things can always be adapted – for instance a healing spell with a Waning Moon could concentrate on banishing the illness, whereas with a Waxing Moon it would be better to visualize increasing wellbeing.

Make a Moon calendar

Using a blank notebook, every night for a month go outside and look up at the Moon. Do a sketch of the Moon you can see, showing what shape it is. Then spend a few minutes focusing on it, connecting with the energy from the Moon itself. Jot down the words, thoughts and feelings that pop into your head. Do this every day, then at the end of the month you can look back and see how your thoughts and feelings corresponded with the phase of the Moon.

Working with the lunar year

Each month has its own particular Moon; they are called by many names. Each month also has its own particular Moon energies too, that you can use to tie in with your Moon magic.

January

Nature spirits: gnomes, brownies
Herbs: marjoram, nuts and cones
Colours: white, violet, black
Stones: garnet, onyx, jet, chrysophrase
Trees: birch
Animals: fox, coyote, pheasant, blue jay

Deities: Freyja, Inanna, Sarasvati, Hera, Ch'ang-O, Sinn

Energies: Sluggish, below the surface, beginning and conceiving, protection, reversing spells. Conserving energy by working on personal problems. Getting your various bodies to work smoothly together for the same goals.

February

Nature spirits: house faeries

Herbs: balm of Gilead, hyssop, myrrh, sage

Colours: light blue, violet

Stones: amethyst, jasper, quartz

Trees: rowan, laurel, cedar

Animals: otter, unicorn, eagle, chickadee

Deities: Brigit, Juno, Kuan Yin, Diana, Demeter, Persephone, Aphrodite

Energies: Energy working toward the surface; purification, growth, healing. Loving the self. Accepting responsibility for past errors, forgiving oneself and making future plans.

March

Nature spirits: merfolk, air and water beings

Herbs: broom, High John root, yellow dock, wood betony, Irish moss

Colours: plate green, violet

Stones: aquamarine, bloodstone

Trees: alder, dogwood

Animals: cougar, hedgehog, boar, sea crow, sea eagle

Deities: Black Isis, the Morrigan, Hecate, Cybele, Astarte, Athena, Minerva, Artemis, Luna

Energies: Energy breaks into the open; growing, prospering, exploring. New beginnings; balance of light and dark. Breaking illusions. Seeing the truth in your life however much it may hurt.

April

Nature spirits: plant faeries

Herbs: basil, chives, dragon's blood, geranium, thistle

Colours: red, gold

Stones: ruby, garnet

Trees: pine, bay, hazel

Animals: bear, wolf, hawk, magpie

Deities: Kali, Hathor, Anahita, Ceres, Ishtar, Venus, Bast

Energies: Put energy into creating and producing; return balance to the nerves. Change, self-confidence, self-reliance. Take advantage of opportunities. Work on temper, emotional flare-ups and selfishness.

May

Nature spirits: faeries, elves

Herbs: dittany of Crete, elder, mint, rose, mugwort, thyme, yarrow

Colours: green, brown, pink

Stones: emerald, malachite, amber, carnelian

Trees: hawthorn

Animals: cat, lynx, leopard, swallow, dove, swan

Deities: Bast, Venus, Aphrodite, Maia, Diana, Artemis, Pan, Horned God

Energies: Full creating energy; propagation. Intuition, contact with faeries and other supernatural beings. Strengthen connection with supernatural protectors and beings around you. Power flowing from nature.

June

Nature spirits: sylphs, zephyrs

Herbs: skullcap, meadowsweet, vervain, tansy, dog grass, parsley, moss

Colours: orange, golden green

Stones: topaz, agate, fluorite

Trees: oak

Animals: monkey, butterfly, frog, toad, wren, peacock

Deities: Aine, Isis, Neith, Green Man, Cerridwen, Ishtar

Energies: Full but restful energy; protect, strengthen and prevent. A time of light; Earth tides are turning. Decision-making, taking responsibility for present happenings. Work on personal inconsistencies. Strengthen and reward yourself for your positive traits.

July

Nature spirits: hobgoblins, faeries of harvested crops

Herbs: honeysuckle, agrimony, lemon balm, hyssop

Colours: silver, blue grey

Stones: pearl, moonstone, white agate

Trees: oak, acacia, ash

Animals: crab, turtle, dolphin, whale, starling, ibis, swallow

Deities: Athena, Juno, Hel, Holda, Cerridwen, Nephthys, Venus

Energies: Relaxed energy; preparing, succeeding. Dreamwork, divination, meditation on goals and plans, especially spiritual ones.

August

Nature spirits: dryads

Herbs: chamomile, St John's wort, bay, angelica, fennel, rue, orange

Colours: yellow, gold

Stones: cat's eye, carnelian, jasper, fire agate

Trees: hazel, alder, cedar

Animals: lion, phoenix, sphinx, dragon, crane, falcon, eagle

Deities: Ganesha, Thoth, Hathor, Diana, Hecate, Nemesis

Energies: Energy into harvesting; gathering, appreciating. Vitality, health, friendships.

September

Nature spirits: trooping faeries

Herbs: copal, fennel, rye, wheat, valerian, skullcap

Colours: brown, yellow green, yellow

Stones: peridot, chrysolite, citrine

Trees: hazel, larch, bay

Animals: snake, jackal, ibis, sparrow

Deities: Demeter, Ceres, Isis, Nephthys, Freyja, Ch'ang-O, Thoth

Energies: Rest after labour; balance of light and dark. Organise. Clean and straighten up physical, mental, emotional and spiritual clutter.

October

Nature spirits: frost faeries, plant faeries

Herbs: pennyroyal, thyme, catnip, angelica, burdock

Colours: dark blue green

Stones: opal, tourmaline, beryl, turquoise

Trees: yew, cypress, acacia

Animals: stag, jackal, elephant, ram, scorpion, heron, crow, and robin

Deities: Ishtar, Astarte, Demeter, Kore, Lakshmi, Horned God, Belili, Hathor

Energies: Energy to let go; inner cleansing. Karma and reincarnation. Justice and balance. Inner harmony.

November

Nature spirits: subterranean faeries

Herbs: verbena, betony, borage, cinquefoil

Colours: grey, sea green

Stones: topaz, lapis lazuli

Trees: alder, cypress

Animals: unicorn, scorpion, crocodile, jackal, owl, goose, sparrow

Deities: Kali, Black Isis, Hecate, Bast, Osiris, Sarasvati, Lakshmi, Mawu

Energies: Take root, prepare. Transformation. Strengthen communication with the deity who seems closest to you.

December

Nature spirits: snow faeries, storm faeries, winter tree faeries

Herbs: holly, ivy, fir, mistletoe

Colours: dark red, white, black

Stones: serpentine, peridot

Trees: pine, fir, holly

Animals: mouse, deer, horse, bear, rook, robin, snowy owl

Deities: Hathor, Hecate, Neith, Athena, Minerva, Ixchel, Osiris, Norns, Fates

Energies: Energy to endure, die, and be reborn; Earth tides turning. Darkness. Personal alchemy. Spiritual paths. Reach out to friends and family, the lonely and needy.

Blue Moon

Nature spirits: banshees and otherworld messengers

Herbs: ginger, hops, hyssop, patchouli, mugwort, nutmeg, star anise

Colours: black, white, purple

Stones: obsidian, onyx, apache tear

Trees: pine, cypress, yew, elder

Animals: bat, wolf, sow, dog, snake, owl, raven, falcon

Deities: Cybele, Hel, Nephthys, Cerridwen, Horned God, Cailleach, Freyja, Holda

Energies: Release and remember; communion with the dead. Prophecy. Releasing old negative memories and emotions.

Moon cords

One way of collecting and keeping Moon energy is by making a Moon cord. The cord is made on a particular phase of the Moon and the energy is trapped in each knot and kept there until needed. So no matter what Moon phase it is, you always have the corresponding Moon energy to work your spell. Of course it is easier and better to do any working on the actual Moon phase, but sometimes it just isn't possible, so if you have Moon cords to hand you don't have to wait.

To make a Moon cord; use wool, string, cord or thread about two feet long. It helps if you have different colours, then you can use a different colour for each phase of the Moon, to help identify them afterwards. You will need to be able to see and feel the energy of the Moon to make your cord. Here, the choice is yours – you can cast a full circle if you wish, otherwise I like to just light a candle and invoke a suitable lunar deity and ask them to lend their power. Face the Moon and hold your cord up towards it. You can say prepared words then, or just ask for what you need – the power of that particular phase of the Moon to be drawn down into your cord for safe keeping until you need it.

You can also use the following:

By knot of ONE, the spell has begun
By knot of TWO, it cometh true
By knot of THREE, so mote it be
By knot of FOUR, this power I store
By knot of FIVE, the spell is alive
By knot of SIX, this spell I fix
By knot of SEVEN, events I'll leaven
By knot of EIGHT, it will be fate
By knot of NINE, what's done is mine

As you visualise the power entering your cord, start tying knots – you will need to tie nine in total, each an equal distance apart. If you don't use the chant above, on your last knot it is an idea to finish with, 'So mote it be'.

Thank the deity and the Moon for their energies.

Keep the cord safe. When you need the energy from that particular Moon phase, place it on your altar, around your candle or wherever you are working your spell.

There are two modes of thought on using the cord. You can either keep using it and just recharge it at the next Moon phase or you can actually undo one of the knots each time you need that energy to release it. Once you have used all the knots you can recharge it.

Lunar oils/herbs

Many herbs and plants are associated with the Moon and her various phases.

Some lunar oils/herbs: aloe, lemon balm, cabbage, camellia, chickweed, coconut, cucumber, eucalyptus, gardenia, grape, passion flower, pea, peach, pear, jasmine, lemon, lettuce, lily, lotus, mallow, myrrh, poppy, potato, sandalwood and willow.

Suggestions for lunar incense blends

Full Moon: frankincense, sandalwood, rose petals
New Moon: jasmine, lemon, lavender
Dark Moon: myrrh, bay, frankincense

Lunar crystals and stones

A lot of crystals also have lunar associations, such as quartz, rose quartz, aquamarine, mother of pearl, moonstone, pearl, beryl, sapphire and hag stones (stones with holes through them). Use a crystal or other stone to make yourself a lunar charm to help keep you in synch with the Moon phases and the phases of your own life.

Chapter 16

Ritual

The first ritual I ever experienced was online in a chat room. And online rituals do work very well, if you have the ability to focus and have an area where you can sit quietly throughout. Online rituals do not work well if you have the children running around behind you and people asking you, 'What's for dinner?' You also need good visualisation skills. They are practical in that if it is raining outside you won't get wet and you don't have to drive anywhere and you don't have to follow directions to a stone circle in the middle of nowhere. You can also attend online rituals wearing your pyjamas and no one points and stares at you. I am not sure how much energy you really get from online rituals to be honest. I like them, don't get me wrong. I do think they are useful and have their place, but I don't think personally they can make you feel the energy a ritual performed in the real world does. Having said that I have been to really good and really bad online and offline ones, it all depends on how well the ritual is written and the energy of those present.

The first ever offline ritual I attended was led by me… boy was I ever scared! A group of people that I met online decided to meet offline at Avebury, which we did and we had a fabulous time. We then scheduled another meet up in Glastonbury with the idea of holding a ritual within the White Springs, which we did and it was lovely. My first offline ritual held outside was one that I attended at Stanton Drew, a lovely old stone circle. It was Imbolc and it was feet numbingly freezing! However, the ritual itself was amazing, with lovely people, a lovely setting, and fabulous energy. I had no idea really what I was doing, but the group performing the ritual were extremely helpful and supportive.

Since then I have attended many rituals and all in beautiful settings – Stonehenge, Knowlton Rings, The Tor in Glastonbury, various beautiful woodland settings and at the ocean shore. But you don't have to have beautiful ancient settings to have a magical ritual. I have also had amazing rituals in my back garden and in my living room. Having a ritual at home means you have the energy from your own personal space. It also means you are warm, dry and have toilet facilities...

There are many different types and styles of ritual. A witch will conduct a ritual differently to that of a druid, for instance, and a hedge witch will have a different idea about ritual to a Wiccan (usually a lot less formal). There are a lot of similarities though and each coven or grove will put their own spin on it. If I am performing a ritual and it is just me on my own I am not formal at all, and usually just say and do whatever comes to mind at the time. I don't use any tools and just go with the flow. If I am performing a ritual with my coven then we still keep it kitchen witchy but we go for a bit more ceremony.

There is a basic outline so I will share with you my template for a ritual. You don't have to use it all – go with what suits you and feels right.

Sweeping the circle

Not everyone does this, but within our Kitchen Witch Coven we like to. You can't separate a witch from her broom! We sweep the circle before we start to dispel any negative energy. The besom bristles never actually touch the ground (you don't want it full of leaves and dirt). It is a symbolic act.

Casting the circle

There are many ways to cast a circle, but generally you (and when I say 'you' in this I mean you on your own, the High Priestess, the High Priest, the Arch Druid etc, whomever is running the show) walk around the circle, whether it is in a field, your garden or your living room, with your arm out chanting the words to cast the circle. (Sometimes if your room is small this might just involve you spinning round on the spot, but that's cool.) You might like to direct the energy by holding an athame, a wand or a sword or you might prefer to just use your finger. As you cast the circle visualise a light 'drawing' a line around the boundary to make a complete circuit. Some also like to visualise the circle becoming a complete dome above you and even becoming a complete sphere like a bubble. The circle you cast is not only to keep out unwanted energy, but also to keep the energy within the circle that you raise in ritual.

Within our coven we sometimes like to cast the circle by sprinkling dried rose petals around the boundary. You could do this with any type of flower or with herbs or salt. (Remember that salt is an herbicide and can damage some surfaces, so only do this where appropriate.)

Calling the quarters

This is the point where you invite the four elements to join your rite. They are invited to lend their particular energies and also to act as guardians. Depending on the type of ritual or pagan tradition, they will be called elements, elementals (used in faerie magic a lot), quarters, guardians or watchtowers. Some will also choose to call upon dragons, animals or archangels to represent the quarters. Most groups start with north then go deosil (clockwise) around the compass, but druids tend to start with the east.

The elements – earth, air, fire and water – correspond to the four compass directions north, east, south and west. Four willing participants from the ritual are usually asked to each call a quarter; if it is a solitary ritual then you call all four. Turn to the compass direction you are calling and request the presence of that particular element. This can be very simple such as: 'I call upon the element of earth, from the north to join my rite today,' or you can make up a chant describing the particular qualities of that element, it is your personal choice.

Invoking deity

Next we invite deity to join us. This can be a general: 'We invite the Lord and Lady to join us today,' or you can invite particular deities to join you. It might be that you would like your patron deities to be with you, you might like to request the presence of deities that align with your intent or you might invite deities that are relevant to the Sabbat or Esbat you are holding the ritual for.

Blessing and consecrating the circle

The circle can be blessed with incense smudging or blessed water. It is done in various ways. A person can walk the circle carrying incense and smudge each individual or they might just smudge the boundary. The same can be done with salt or blessed water. It is a way of cleansing the people within the circle and purifying any negative energy.

The body of the ritual

It is at this point that the main part of the ritual happens. What happens will depend on the group, the reason for meeting, the time of year etc. Usually the main person will speak about why everyone is there. For instance, if it is to celebrate a Sabbat then they will talk about what the Sabbat means and why everyone celebrates it.

The working

If you are a solitary then chances are you have done all the processes so far in order to work a spell. If so, this is the time when you would perform that spell. Some group rituals will work a spell at this point too.

Energy

Some groups will also spend some time raising energy. It might be done in the form of a chant or a hum. Druids raise energy chanting the Awen, and it might be done with drumming, singing or dancing. The energy raised is usually directed by the High Priestess into a cone in the centre of the circle. When the energy has reached its peak it will be released and sent to wherever it needs to go. It might be for healing, for instance, so will be sent out into the universe to be delivered where it is needed. If you are a solitary you can also raise energy. My favourite way is to use a drum beat, but singing and dancing work well too.

Wine and bread

A lot of groups choose to share wine and bread within ritual. Our coven usually uses fruit juice (in case there are children present) and cake or cookies. Well, let's face it, cake is much nicer than bread! One of our group will walk around the circle with a chalice of juice and offer it to each person to take a sip. As they do they will say, 'May you never thirst.' The same is done with the cake, but this time the bearer of goodies will say, 'May you never hunger.' Each and every person is offered the drink and food.

Talking stick

I have been at lots of rituals where a 'talking stick' is passed around. I have to admit we don't do this at our Kitchen Witch Coven rituals because some people get completely freaked out at the thought of having to say words out loud in front of others. But most groups never expect you to use the talking stick if you don't want to. It is perfectly acceptable to just pass the stick onto the next person without saying a word. The talking stick is passed from person to person, when it is your turn to hold the stick you can say a few words. It might just be, 'Thank you for letting me attend.'

Closing

And that's about it for the body of the ritual. Now, to close, you do the whole 'setting up' process in reverse. You thank the deities for joining you and bid them farewell, you then do the same with the quarters, thanking them (in reverse order). Then you walk widdershins (anti clockwise) around the circle to uncast it.

It is at this point that you should really ground yourself. Sometimes a lot of energy is raised in a ritual, even if you have just been performing a solitary ritual. Clap your hands, stamp your feet or put the palms of your hands on the ground and allow any excess energy to direct itself back into the Earth.

Chapter 17

Spell Working

In reality I don't believe spell working to be a huge part of being a witch. I don't do spells at the drop of a hat, not even a black pointy one. I am not constantly standing over my cauldron, cackling with eye of newt and wing of bat ready to drop into the bubbling mixture contained therein.

I do believe a good witch will try to find a mundane solution first before resorting to spell work.

However, I do work simple candle spells regularly. Such as lighting a white candle for peace when there has been a natural disaster in the world or a big accident, for instance. I do light a blue candle if a friend is poorly and has asked for healing. I generally keep it simple. I do also like to work with medicine bags and witches bottles, but more about them later.

The most important 'ingredient' in a spell is intent. You have to know exactly what it is you want to achieve and you have to be specific. Spells have a nasty habit of acting in a totally unpredictable way, I know from experience. Having said that, the only way you can improve your spell working skill is with practice.

Firstly decide why you are doing the spell, what is the outcome that you are hoping to achieve and have you done all you can on the mundane level to work it out/sort it out etc.

Be very specific with your intent. For instance I had a lot of mishaps with banishing spells in the past. If I was having trouble with situations in my life I would work a banishing spell to rid my life of all negativity – expecting the one person or the one situation to disappear off into the sunset (still alive and still with all their limbs I might add) and that life would be much brighter and better for me. What I hadn't counted on and what took me some time and several banishing spells to realise is that banishing

ALL negativity really does mean ALL and also includes unexpected people or situations in your life. Not only did the person or situation I was aiming at drift away, so did various other people. While in the long run it has proved to all work out for the best, at the time I was totally confused with what transpired and was in a total state of chaos for some time. Be mindful of the old saying, 'Be careful what you wish for'. Banishing anything from your life also leaves a void and that void tends to hanker after being filled with something and that something is usually very similar to that which was banished in the first place. So also be mindful that if you do banish something make a contingency to fill that void with something good and positive.

I would also ask you to be mindful when working a love spell. While you may want to draw the man or woman of your dreams to you (which is OK to wish for), I would warn against naming them or directing your love spell to a specific person – that is going against another person's free will. If it happened that he or she came to be with you, would you always wonder whether you had trapped them with magic or whether they did really love you? Sometimes it can backfire…

Do you need to cast a circle before working a spell? There are different schools of thought on this and I must admit I don't tend to. My house is very well protected already and my spells are usually only for healing, luck, prosperity etc – if your plan is to call forth daemons or spirits then it probably would be safer to cast a circle first.

What do you need? There are many different types of spells; a basic spell might just involve standing outside looking up at the Moon and making a wish. A spell can also involve candles, herbs, crystals and the like. Not usually eye of newt and wing of bat, but these are actually old folk names for herbs so the newt and bat population can heave a sigh of relief. (Eye of newt is mustard seed and wing of bat is holly.)

Be prepared. Work out your intent first, what type of spell you want to use, what ingredients or items you will need and get them all ready. Write out any words that you want to say. Lay out everything first. It's a bit embarrassing to work a grand spell, call upon deity, light candles, sprinkle herbs and then realise you have forgotten one of the vital ingredients…

Be careful when wording your request. If you are in need of money, only ask for what you need and also ask for ways in which you can earn it or do something in exchange for it. A request of, 'I want to be a millionaire,' probably won't work as well as, 'I would like to find myself in a situation to earn enough money to cover all my bills'. I also personally like to add 'and harm to none' on the end of my spells, just as a cover-all clause. The old familiar example used is that of working a spell for lots of money and then your favourite relation dropping dead the next day – you might inherit lots of money but someone you love has lost their life in the process – and we don't want that happening!

Whilst you are working your spell, keep the goal or desire in your mind and visualise it all coming to fruition.

If you want to add power to your spell check the correspondences – use herbs that have the same intent, work your spell on the day of the week that has the same intent, check the time of day, the Moon phase and even the planetary phase. Each one of these alignments will add power to your working.

Days of the week: spell working correspondences

Monday: the Moon's day, inspiration, illusions, psychic abilities, emotions and dreams

Tuesday: justice, bravery, strength, sports and aggression.

Wednesday: communication, intelligence, creativity, the arts, wisdom, business plans

Thursday: abundance, prosperity, healing, leadership

Friday: love, romance, friendships, happiness and passion

Saturday: spiritual cleansing, protection, removing obstacles, banishing negativity

Sunday: the Sun's day, personal power, healing, achieving your goals, success, personal growth

Anger

Don't work a spell if you are angry, this is a bad move. Anger is a very strong emotion and can taint and colour your working in a way that you might not expect or ultimately like. It is easier to calm down and then work a spell correctly than work one in anger and have to undo it later.

Candle spells

With candle spells I also like to follow the rule that a candle should only be used for one specific spell. If you work a love spell with a pretty pink candle and only burn it half way, don't then use that candle for another intent. The spells tend to get mixed up and confused. I would suggest one spell per candle and always burn the candle fully, that way you know the spell has worked fully and the magic has been released. It is safer to burn a spell candle a bit at a time for the same spell rather than leave it burning unattended, but it is best to burn it entirely in one go if you have the time to keep an eye on it. If you have any candle stubs left, bury them in the garden.

Spells can also take the form of witches bottles, medicine bags and poppets – more about those later!

Chapter 18

The Elements

The five elements are very important within witchcraft. Earth, air, fire, water and spirit make up the elements. Each one has its own unique energy and characteristics.

Earth

When I think of earth I think about soil. Soil contains and keeps all the minerals and moisture that all the plants on the planet need to live. Earth is everything we are and everything we have comes from the element of earth. We are born of it and we return to it at the end of our lives. Earth is the foundation, so it is no wonder that the element of earth is associated with abundance and prosperity. Earth also stabilises and grounds us. Think of the grounding exercise mentioned earlier – it involves not only trees that grow, but the earth, soil and rock of the planet.

Earth is associated with north, with the season of winter and the advancement of old age. Winter, for me at least, is a time of reflecting. The trees and plants and even the animals have all withdrawn into Mother Earth to recuperate, to replenish, ready to venture forth in the spring, renewed and refreshed.

Don't forget to look after this element, the planet, the environment around you. It can even be something small like picking up a piece of litter.

Earth has the colours of the season of winter, those of the dark nights, brown soil, dark grassy landscape and the white of frost and snow. It is also the time of the Cailleach; she is the Goddess of Winter.

To represent this element you could use a small dish of soil, an earthenware dish, a stone, a pebble, a crystal or even a piece of wood.

Air

When I think of the element of air I get an image of a bright blue sky with wispy white clouds in my mind. The sky is limitless; you can't see an end to it.

Air is all about intellect, truth and knowledge. Air means truth, truth in who you really are and the freedom that comes with that realisation.

Think about the qualities of the wind too, when it whips up the leaves and sends them dancing around; when a wisp of breeze catches your hair. There is nothing quite like the feeling of standing on top of a windy hill with your arms outstretched just letting the wind wrap around you. Don't forget that air also has its destructive side, think of hurricanes and tornadoes.

Air represents east, the season of spring and youth. It is the place of hope and new beginnings. We get up, we start each new day fresh with opportunities to learn and grow. We go out into the world to go about our business.

Spring has the same feeling – fresh, new energy. We have hibernated over winter, dreaming and planning. Now it is time to put those plans into action.

Youth is an exciting and even slightly scary time. We set out on our own, starting to explore the big world for ourselves. New experiences, new people, new ventures. This is the time when we start to discover who we are.

Air is associated with thoughts. We need air to breathe, and therefore to live. The air we breathe in allows us to think clearly, to clear our minds.

Air has the colours of spring: the yellow of the rising sun, the light blue of the sky and white of the clouds. Even the pale green of new foliage and the pink of blossom; the pale colours of Bride, the Goddess of Spring.

To represent the element of air you might like to use feathers, incense or spring flowers.

Fire

When I think of fire I visualise a huge bonfire, glowing red, yellow and orange; a huge pile of crackling logs and sticks. I can hear spitting sparks of flame and feel the heat on my face.

Fire brings warmth, comfort and protection. It is the light in the dark that drives away outside threats. Fire brings people together as a community. Although most houses now don't have open fires in each room, a lot still have fireplaces. The hearth is the centre of a home.

Fire is passion; it is the burning flame inside that gives us energy and strength. It is the fire within us that helps us meet the challenges life brings to us. Fire also sparks our imagination, lights our passions and fills us with enthusiasm and encouragement.

Fire can also be destructive, but from that destruction comes renewal and rebirth – think of the Phoenix rising from the ashes. The warning that comes with fire is that it does need to be kept in check. A fire that causes rage can get out of hand.

Cast your mind to the blacksmith's forge. The blacksmith takes raw material, heats it in the fire and creates something new from it. A transformation, this we can do with our own selves.

The fire within you is your own personal power. It is the force that gives you confidence. It takes away fear and challenges you to push yourself that bit further.

Fire represents the south, the season of summer and adulthood. The Sun is at its highest point. Summer is when we put all our energy into projects and help them to grow and mature. The projects that were started in the spring are now flourishing. It is a time for energy, activity and passion. A time to laugh, dance, sing and have fun.

Adults have experience, experience of life and who they are. By adulthood you should have found your place in the world. You have responsibilities, control of your life and your expectations. Just remember to enjoy yourself too, find your inner passion and run with it!

Fire is the colour of summer: the reds of a beautiful sunset, the yellow of the Sun and even the green and bright colours of summer flowers and plants. I think of Belenos the Celtic Sun God.

To represent fire the most obvious item is a candle, especially a red one. You could also use a red stone or crystal.

Water

With water my first thought is always of the ocean, of waves crashing on the shore.

What would we do without water? It sustains all life. Without water we and all the plants and animals would not survive. Water is very powerful – the ocean, a flood, a tidal wave.

Water is all about emotions. Emotions flow, chop and change and rise to the surface as water does in a river, lake or ocean. A shower of rain can be refreshing like the release of emotion or destructive like the waves on a rough sea.

Water is also cleansing and healing. We clean ourselves, wash our food, and clean our houses and possessions with water. Your daily household chores such as washing up can be cleansing rituals in themselves.

Water is excellent for scrying. Divination with water uses our intuition, imagination and emotions. Take a bowl that has a dark inside, fill it with water and drop a silver coin in the bottom. Calm and centre yourself, look into the water and see what images come to you.

Water represents the west. It is the season of autumn and old age. This is the time of harvest, a time to gather in. What we have spent the year nurturing and tending to is now ready to reap. It is time to let go.

As people get older and become more aware of their mortality, they seek to balance their lives. They surrender some of the hard work they have been doing and concentrate on what is most important to them. Often these are things that bring emotional fulfilment, like spending time with loved ones, or pursuing a creative dream.

Water gives us the flow of our emotions and nurtures our lives. In return, we can offer it our love. Everything we do with love, and every act of love we perform, honours water. Love, like water, has the power of healing.

The colours of water are the colours of the sea, lakes and rivers: the blue of the Mediterranean, and the grey of the North Sea, the black of a deep lake and the green of the sea before a storm. But they are also all the glorious colours of the autumn leaves that remind me of the God Mabon.

On my altar a bowl with sea shells represents water.

Spirit

There is the fifth element, that of spirit. To me it encompasses all the others, it is all and it is nothing.

What are the elements for?

Elements are used in ritual, in spells, and in our everyday lives. They make us who we are. We use them in ritual and spell work to bring their own particular characteristics and energies. But each of us is made up from varying amounts of each element. By balancing the four elements within us we can balance our lives.

How do you find out what element type you are?

On a piece of paper make four columns for each of the elements – earth, air, fire and water. Under each heading write the name of something in your environment that strikes you as being closely related to that element. Other people, even characteristics of your own personality might remind you of that particular element. Write down anything that comes to mind. When you have finished your list, look for overlaps between the elements.

Then think about the various aspects of your life – home,

family, friends, work, school, commuting, exercising, sports, hobbies, bad habits, strengths, weaknesses etc.

Once you have a completed list take a look and see if any one area of your life seems weighted more toward one element than the others. This isn't bad! Most of us have a special affinity for one or two of the elements.

Count the number of entries in each column and compare them. Just how weighted toward one element is your list? Can you think of other things in your life that you are leaving off the list that might fall under the other elements?

Working with the elements

If you can't get outside to work with the elements directly, work with the crystals suggested – meditate using them and visualise the element itself. Draw a picture of an elemental, print one from the internet or look in a book at an image of the elemental for each element and meditate. Research the animals that are associated with each element. Pick one or two of the scents that are associated with each element and wear them.

For each activity you do, make a mental note of how it feels, how you think you are connecting with that element, what smells there are, what you sense.

Earth

Earthy activities include gardening, cooking, walking in the forest, walking across fields, mountain climbing, visiting a garden or a garden centre, working with herbs, recycling, picking up litter, plunging your hands or feet into fresh earth.

Air

To experience air, go outside when it is windy and let the air blow through you, sit on top of a hill or mountain, check the air quality in your area, or open a window. Fly a kite, watch the birds, lie on your back and watch the clouds, burn incense.

Fire

To enjoy the element of fire, have a bonfire or a BBQ, meditate watching a candle flame, sit and watch an open fire, watch fireworks.

Water

Go swimming, splash in puddles, walk in the rain, visit a pond or the seashore, wash the car, water the plants, take a bath or a shower to connect with the essence of water.

Chapter 19

Chakras

Tied in with energy are chakras.

There are seven main chakras, but there are a lot more which you can investigate if working with chakras interests you.

A chakra is essentially a spinning wheel of energy that lies along your spine. The seven major ones lie along the vertical spinal axis from the crown of your head to your base. They can vary in size depending on how active they are, and they vary in how fast or slow they spin. The size and spinning depends on how balanced, cleansed, open or shut they are.

Each chakra corresponds to a specific colour of the rainbow, parts of the body and areas of consciousness.

They are really junctions that send spiritual energy around your body and your mind. They connect your physical, mental and spiritual aspects, affecting your wellbeing.

You can use visualisation and meditate to work with your chakras; you can also aid this by working with crystals that correspond to each chakra.

Base chakra

Your base chakra is red and is located at the base of your spine; although I am also of the school of thought that this chakra can 'float' anywhere between the base of your spine and your feet, but go with what feels right to you.

It is associated with basic health and survival. This chakra keeps you grounded and is your link to reality. When this chakra is unbalanced it will affect you ability to connect spiritually, mentally and physically. Your base chakra is also the key to your kundalini, the fire spirit within your body.

Sacral chakra

This chakra is orange and is located just below your naval. This chakra is associated with emotions, vitality, fertility, reproduction and sexual energy.

Solar plexus chakra

The solar plexus chakra is yellow in colour and is located just above your naval and corresponds with your digestive organs. It affects your will power and your energy centre. This chakra houses your personal power, action, empowerment and your ego.

Heart chakra

Your heart chakra is green in colour and is located pretty much where your real heart lies, just in the centre of your chest. This chakra is associated with affairs of the heart – love, compassion and affection.

Throat chakra

The throat chakra is blue in colour and you will find it at the base of your neck. It is associated with your vocal cords, communication and creative expression.

Third eye chakra

Your third eye or brow chakra is indigo in colour and is found in the spot just between your eyebrows. This chakra corresponds with your inner vision, your psychic abilities and your imagination. It is also related to your pituitary gland. This chakra is your connection to the inner and outer worlds.

Crown chakra

The crown chakra is violet in colour and can be found at the top of your head. It is associated with the pineal gland, enlightenment and your connection with the divine.

Exercise to open your chakras

Make yourself comfortable, I find that lying on the floor or the bed is easiest. You can also place some crystals around you if you would like to. Close your eyes and focus on your breathing.

As you breathe in, visualise a bright, white cleansing and purifying light; as you breathe out send out all the negative energies.

Once you are calm and peaceful, visualise a white light above your head, allow this light to flow down into your crown chakra, as it meets your chakra visualise the light turning to a beautiful violet colour. Open your chakra by visualising it as a lotus flower, each petal opening and in the centre a violet spinning ball of energy. As the petals of the crown chakra lotus open, it opens your spirituality.

Then allow the light from above your head to travel down further to your third eye chakra. As it meets the chakra the light turns to an indigo blue. The chakra becomes an orchid flower. It starts as a bud and then opens out and blossoms to reveal a spinning ball of indigo light. This also opens your ability for telepathy and clairvoyance.

The light then goes to your throat chakra. As the light meets this it turns into a beautiful bright blue colour and becomes a cornflower. As the petals open you see inside a ball of swirling blue energy. As this flower chakra blossoms it opens your ability for clairaudience.

The light then moves down further to your heart chakra. As the light meets this chakra it turns a bright green colour and becomes a rose bud. As the petals open, you see inside a ball of swirling green energy. This opens up your ability to feel, your sensitivity, love and awareness, your psychic power and your understanding.

The light moves on to your solar plexus. As the light meets this chakra it turns a bright yellow colour. As it touches the chakra it turns into a sunflower. The sunflower blooms and in the centre is a spinning ball of yellow energy. This is the centre of your power. As the flower blossoms it opens your strength and determination, it helps you to fulfilment.

The light travels down to your sacral chakra. As the light meets this chakra it turns a bright orange colour and becomes the bud of a poppy flower. As each petal opens, the poppy reveals a ball of orange spinning energy in its centre. As this chakra opens, so does your centre of psychic power.

Further down the light travels to your base chakra. As the light meets this one it turns a bright red colour and becomes the roots of a tree. As the roots grow your chakra opens to become a ball of swirling red energy. This chakra opens to reveal your ability to ground and centre, to remain connected to the Earth. Visualise these roots travelling down into the Earth. As they do so they draw energy up into your body.

Spend a few moments watching these colours of energy swirl around as they heal, soothe and energise your spiritual and physical body.

Now visualise all of the colours forming together to make a protection shield around you, like a bubble. This shield will protect you from negative energies.

Once this is done, slowly, gradually come back to the present.

Stretch your arms and legs and clap your hands. Take some time to do this, don't stand up straight away. It is usually a good idea to have a cup of tea or eat something after this type of exercise.

Make your own set of chakra balancing stones

Choose seven crystals, each one to represent an individual chakra. There are some suggestions below but go with what feels right for you. You can use different crystals or you could use seven quartz crystals.

Take each crystal in your power hand, one at a time, 'charge' it with energy and ask that it be connected to a particular chakra. You might use a quartz crystal for your crown chakra, take it in your hand and visualise it being filled with clear white light. As you visualise this, say something like, 'In the name of the

Divine/God and Goddess/Lord and Lady I ask that this crystal be charged with energy and connected to my crown chakra.' Do this with each crystal.

Keep these crystals separate and only use them for working with your chakras. Cleanse and charge them regularly.

When you do a chakra cleansing/opening/balancing meditation place each one of the crystals on the corresponding chakra position on your body to allow their energy to cleanse and recharge each one of your chakras.

Chakra crystals

Crystals for the crown: quartz, amethyst, danburite, chalcopyrite, moonstone, selenite

Crystals for the third eye: lapis lazuli, amethyst, sodalite, charolite, sugilite, lepidolite

Crystals for the throat: blue lace agate, blue chalcedony, sodalite, turquoise, angelite

Crystals for the heart: chrysocolla, amazonite, malachite, aventurine, rose quartz, peridot

Crystals for the solar plexus: citrine, yellow jasper, calcite, topaz, amber, sunstone

Crystals for the sacrum: carnelian, imperial topaz, fire agate, fire opal, orange calcite

Crystals for root: ruby, garnet, red jasper, bloodstone, red aventurine

Chakra oils

You can use essential oils to aid chakra work too. Use a dab of corresponding oil on each chakra spot or wear a particular oil as a perfume if one of your chakras is unbalanced or burn chakra-related oils on an oil burner while doing your balancing meditation.

Root chakra oils: benzoin, cedarwood, frankincense, myrrh, patchouli, vetiver

Sacral chakra oils: bergamot, cardamom, clary sage, neroli, orange, ylang ylang

Solar plexus oils: black pepper, cinnamon, clove, coriander, geranium, ginger, grapefruit

Heart chakra oils: jasmine, lavender, rose, ylang ylang, geranium, mandarin

Throat chakra oils: basil, chamomile, cypress, peppermint, spearmint

Third eye chakra oils: angelica, bay, juniper, marjoram, rosemary

Crown chakra oils: sandalwood, rose, neroli, myrrh, lavender, jasmine, frankincense

Learning the names

To help you remember the names of the chakras and their details, make some flash cards.

On each card draw or write the name of the flower associated with the chakra, colour it in the appropriate colour, then add the key details and their names.

If you also have corresponding crystals to hand, lay the flash cards out in a line in the correct order and place the correct crystal with each card, this will help you remember them.

Then mix the cards up and lay them out again in the right order, do this until you have memorised the correct sequence. It might take a few goes it might take a few days to learn them. Don't rush it.

You can use flash cards to help you remember all sorts of things, such as herbs and their uses or crystals and their properties.

Chapter 20

Auras

What is an aura? Well, an aura is an energy field that surrounds every living thing. Once you can see an aura you will see that it is made up of different colours. The colour of an aura is dependent on the mood, emotion, mind set and health of a person (or plant or animal).

When you interact with someone else your aura will also react with theirs. If you are close enough you will get an instant feeling – a like or a dislike.

It might take some practice to be able to see auras, but it is an interesting exercise to undertake and can give you lots of insight not only into yourself but others as well.

There are several layers to each aura:

Astral aura

This extends about 8 to 12 inches from your body and is usually rainbow coloured. This layer is the astral connection between the physical and the spiritual world.

Etheric aura

This extends about 12 to 24 inches from your body and is usually blue in colour. This layer relates to our physical being and awareness of our body.

Celestial aura

This extends about 24 inches from your body and is usually made up of pastel colours. This layer is our connection to the spiritual world.

Ketheric aura

This extends 36 to 48 inches from your body and is usually a golden colour. This layer is the outer layer of your aura and protects all the other layers within it.

How to see an aura

Try this exercise, it might take a bit of practice, keep trying – don't give up!

Lay in a comfortable position in a dark or low-lit room.

Hold your hands out in front of you. Don't focus on them, but just casually gaze at them. Move your hands slowly in front of you, gently bringing your fingers together so they almost touch. You should, with practice, be able to see a faint blue shimmer around your fingers. This is the etheric aura that you are seeing.

Another exercise is to stand in front of a mirror, look at your reflection and then close your eyes, squeeze them really tightly shut then spring them open. For a split second or two you should see a coloured shimmer around your reflection.

Try placing a piece of white paper on a flat surface and holding your hand on the paper. Let your eyes relax their focus, slowly you should see a coloured shimmer around your hand.

Practice these exercises; be patient, it may take some time.

You can also try these exercises on willing human volunteers, but also try it on pets, plants and rocks.

The following are the more common colours and what they symbolise in the aura:

Red: symbolises strength, passion, and will. Can also mean nervousness and a quick temper.

Orange: symbolises warmth, thoughtfulness, and creativity. Can also show pride, self control or vanity, depending on the shade of orange.

Yellow: symbolises mental activity and optimism. Can also mean shyness or wisdom.

Green: symbolises sympathy and calm. Darker green can mean jealousy; light green can be the sign of a healer.

Blue: symbolises quiet and calm. Blue auras are good ones to have. Blue is the colour of spirituality, but can also be a sign of a moody person.

Indigo and violet: these colours indicate someone who is a seeker and a practical person.

Black: a colour of protection, but can also mean that the person is keeping secrets.

Pink: symbolises love and compassion.

White: symbolises purity and truth.

Brown: indicates someone who is grounded.

Black spots: these can mean the person is imbalanced about something or that they have negative habits that need work.

Aura cleansing

Aura cleansing is an activity which is good to perform daily. It is a good one to do while in the shower.

Visualize a white light coming down and flowing through your body and out into your aura, cleansing and purifying it.

Chapter 21

Affirmations

Affirmations – do you use them? Even if you think you don't, I bet you do!

Affirmations are simple statements that we make, positive or negative. They can be made on purpose when we want to change some aspect of our life. They may also be made automatically without even thinking about it – for instance when we tell ourselves, 'Oh I am no good at that'.

What we say, positive or negative, affects our behaviour.

In order to change your situation and create a new reality, you have to bombard your subconscious mind with positive thoughts. This is where affirmations come into play...

'I will live each day to the fullest'
'I am strong, confident and wonderful'
'Today and always, I am patient, kind and generous'
'I am worth it'
'I am in total control of my destiny'
'My life is full of love and happiness'

They all sound pretty positive don't they?

But what about the ones we do without thinking? Take a moment and think about the things you say automatically:

'I can't do that'
'I am no good at that'
'That is too scary'
'I can't attend that as I don't like crowds'

I bet you make these statements, or variations of them, all the time without thinking.

See if you can catch yourself doing it. Pay attention to what you say and how you say it. Stop yourself and see if you can turn the negative comment into a positive affirmation.

You will be surprised how effective it is.

Start your day with a couple of positive affirmations. Stop a few times throughout your day and think about what you have said or thought – was it positive or negative?

You have the power!

Chapter 22

Book of Shadows

The Book of Shadows is often called a grimoire too. This is a witch's record book. What you put into it and what other witches put into theirs will differ with each person.

My own Book of Shadows is a large lever arch file that contains sections on deities I have worked with, correspondences and information on oils, incenses, herbs and crystals. I keep copies of all the rituals that I have been a part of, meditations I have written or ones that I have liked, along with details on auras, divination, totems I have worked with, chakras, Sabbats, Esbats and colour magic. It is my reference book and also a history of sorts of my journey along this path.

Some witches will also use their Book of Shadows as a journal or diary, writing about their experiences within its pages as a record of personal memories to look back on. I am a bit useless at keeping a journal so it is not something I have ever done. On occasion when I have been gifted a pretty blank journal I get inspired and write for a couple of days, but I don't have the will power to keep it going. If you want to give it a try though, journaling can be extremely therapeutic and enlightening. Initially start by writing a couple of pages a day, write whatever is in your head. It doesn't matter about the grammar or the spelling or even if your writing makes sense or not, just empty your thoughts, feelings and emotions onto the pages. This also works well if you find you can't sleep at night because your brain is too active. Try writing down everything that you are thinking about. Sometimes just getting it out of your head can calm your mind enough to sleep peacefully.

I am sure most of us would love to have a big old leather-bound tome for a Book of Shadows, but in reality they are expensive and you have to hand write it all – I am way to lazy for that! But if you are happy to write by hand they do look beautiful, and you can use all sorts of coloured and scented inks to write with.

I have printed all the pages in my Book of Shadows from the computer, but I do hand decorate each page before I add it. I use coloured pens and pencils, stickers and sometimes a bit of fancy glitter. I draw designs and stencil shapes around the margin of each page corresponding my images to the subject matter.

Some witches I know keep their entire Book of Shadows on the computer, which is perfectly fine and makes searching for information very easy – just make sure to back up regularly.

I have seen the system where a Book of Shadows is made up of several books – each one on a different subject within the Craft, which works very well too.

I find that lever arch files are very suitable. You can cover and decorate the outside and you can change it around, add and remove pages very easily.

At the end of the day what you put in your Book of Shadows, how you create it and design it, is entirely up to you. It is after all a very personal item.

Chapter 23

Divination

Does the word divination conjure up for you a picture of a gypsy in a headscarf wearing big gold hoop earrings, poring over a crystal ball? Reading a crystal ball is just a very small part of divination, there are many, many other methods.

But what does the word mean?

The dictionary says:

1. *The practice of attempting to foretell future events or discover hidden knowledge by occult or supernatural means*
2. *Augury: prophecy*
3. *Perception by intuition; instinctive foresight*

Which pretty much covers it!

But it's not just about shuffling a set of tarot cards and pulling out one or two, there is a lot more to it. It is about connecting with the divine, connecting with spirit guides, connecting with our psychic abilities. We have to be able to make this connection to have the insights revealed to us. It is a very special and very sacred experience.

The symbolic images in divination activate and speak to a deep intuitive part of ourselves which the logical, conscious mind cannot understand or control. This part of ourselves is known as the subconscious. This subconscious aspect of being represents our inner self, those deep, highly personal feelings and qualities which provide the foundation for our entire being and give us the motivation behind our behaviour, thoughts, emotions, etc. The subconscious is that part of us that just 'knows' to do something. It is the source of flashes of inspiration and creative expression.

Why work with divination?

We can use divinatory means to get answers, to seek knowledge, wisdom, guidance and insight. But we must remember to actually listen or really see and understand what is being shown to us, and if it shows the future we must also remember that the future is not set in stone. Divination can only show us possible outcomes. But it is a very useful tool nonetheless, for guiding us and giving us answers and options. It is extremely useful if you have a dilemma and don't know what to do. It can show you alternatives, give you suggestions and options you may not have thought of.

I would caution that if you are reading for others it is advisable never to predict death, destruction or desperate unhappiness. There are ways of hinting and guiding them away from a situation you see or leading them to realisation, but never drop a complete bombshell on them. I would also advise never to perform a reading for someone else other than the seeker. If someone comes to you and asks for a reading for their mother, brother, neighbour etc then don't. It is up to the person themselves to seek you out.

Always keep the positive in mind, because the outcome of most things, if not all, can be changed or at least shifted. If a person has come to you for a reading then they are usually looking for some guidance or help. Sending them away with foretelling of doom and gloom is irresponsible, unethical and actually downright mean. Offer them the information from the reading, but offer them the information with hope and a positive outlook, keep them on the up.

What to use

Oh so many choices! But be warned once you start with something like tarot or oracle cards, you will usually end up with lots; there is always one more beautiful set of cards that needs to come home with you ;-).

The divination tools, such as cards or a crystal ball, act as channels or keys to our own inner psychic abilities. You will probably find as you experiment with various types that you will instantly connect with some but not 'get' others at all. I love using tarot and oracle cards but have never been able to connect with runes. It will be slightly different for everyone.

And, of course, you don't actually need to purchase anything to perform divination, there are lots of divination tools in nature too.

Here is a look at some common and perhaps some more uncommon types:

Tarot cards

Tarot is a deck of 78 cards, all with their own individual meanings. There are 21 trump or major arcana cards. These all follow the journey of the Fool throughout the major events of his life. The remaining cards make up the minor arcana, which are separated into four suits, each suit representing an element and aspect of life. Swords are air and intellect, wands are fire and passion, cups are water and emotion and disks/pentacles are earth and material. Each number also has a meaning. The court cards follow the suits, but each represents a person, the querent or their personality.

Although there are many different designs of tarot cards the basic meanings for each card remain the same throughout the sets.

You can do many different types of readings by using different spreads such as a simple three-card spread for the past, present and future, a seven-card spread for each day of the week to come, a twelve-card spread for the year ahead and so many other permutations.

Oracle cards

These are cards like the tarot and seem to be usually in sets of around 44 to 54 cards, but each set will have different meanings. It will all depend on the person who designed them. They can be read in spreads like the tarot i.e. past, present or future, but work very well for 'a card a day' – you draw a card in the morning to see what the day holds in store for you.

Runes

Generally associated with Norse traditions, the runes are a set of symbols. The runes can be read for divination or can be drawn on talismans and amulets, wands, staffs, athames or candles to add power. The most well known rune system is the Elder Futhark. You can purchase sets of runes from occult shops and online, but they are very easy to make – use pebbles from the beach, the little round glass stones used in floristry or discs of wood cut from small tree branches. Paint the rune signs on them.

Lithomancy

Divination using stones, crystals, bones, shells – collected in the hands, shaken and thrown. Each item will have a meaning and where it lands will also bear relevance to the reading. These are really easy to make and you can use all sorts of things.

Ogham

Ancient Celtic system using the symbolism of trees. Again these are easy to make yourself, you can collect a twig from each of the trees in the Ogham, but that isn't always easy. Use twigs from a favourite tree local to you or you could even use lolly sticks; paint the ogham symbol on each one.

Crystal ball

This type of divination is done using a quartz crystal in a sphere shape, usually with a candle to help see shapes and images. Scry on the surface of the ball to see what messages you get from the images. Scrying with crystals is also called crystallomancy. For this you can use any shape of crystal; it doesn't have to be a sphere.

Scrying mirror

You can use any mirrored surface to scry, but traditionally black mirrors are used. Again, using candle light will help bring images to you.

Reading tea leaves

This is one of the traditional ways of divination. Using loose leaf tea, the reader will swirl the leaves in the bottom of the cup to see how they move and tip them out on to a saucer to see what images arise. The official name for reading tea leaves is tasseomancy or tasseography. You can also do this using coffee grounds.

Wax shapes

Officially called ceroscopy, a reader will light a candle, ask a question and then drip wax from it onto a bowl of cold water. The answer to the query can be read in the shapes and images of the wax.

Water scrying

This is one of my favourite ways to scry. You can scry very easily by using a bowl with a dark inner filled with water; it helps to drop a shiny silver coin in the bottom. You read the images you see on the surface. You can also add to this by dropping ink or herbs on the top of the water. This is called hydromancy. If you drop a stone into a pond or well you can also read the ripples caused, this is called pegomancy. Scrying works best if done when it is dark and by having a lighted candle beside the bowl to add some movement to the surface of the water, or better still put the bowl in view of the Full Moon.

Pyromancy

Another one of my favourites! Reading messages in the flames of fire. You can do this with a bonfire, fire in a grate or chimenea or even with a candle flame. I like to throw in a sprinkle of herbs to help. You can also use the smoke from a fire to divine with too.

Dowsing

Using a pendulum or divining rods. Pendulums are really easy to make, you just need a piece of thread, string or leather thong, add a small heavy object to the end such as a hag stone, piece of wood or a shell and you have a readymade pendulum.

Chapter 24

Crystals

Crystals have so many uses within the Craft. Each individual crystal has its own properties and energies.

Attuning to a crystal

I like this exercise to get the feel of the stones I have in my collection.

Hold the chosen stone/metal in the palm of your hand and close your eyes. Breathe deeply, sending all of your senses toward the stone. Open up to feel and hear the stone's vibrations. What does it say to you? What feelings and impressions do you get from it? How does the stone make you feel? All of your answers will be useful to you when you work with the stone in the future, make a note of what you got from each one to refer back to if you need to. There are lots of crystal correspondences in books and on the net, but I always feel that your own personal ones work the best.

Crystals are good for making grids, mandalas and medicine wheels. Use a flat plate or cloth and put it in an area that won't be disturbed. Pick crystals intuitively that are right for your intent. You may, for instance, want to make a prosperity grid. Lay out the stones in a grid shape or a mandala pattern; go with what feels right. Charge each crystal with your intent. Leave the grid or mandala in place for as long as you feel it is needed. You can touch the crystals to recharge them if you feel they require it.

Healing with crystals

You can make a healing grid as described above, but you can also use crystals to make medicine bags for healing. Gather together as few or as many crystals as you feel is right, charge them with your intent and pop them in a small bag – give the bag to the person in need of healing or leave it on your altar with the intent of healing for that person.

Crystals can also be used for healing on the body. Pick a crystal that you know is good for healing, or pick one by intuition. Place it on the area of the body that needs curing and work with the energy within the crystal to aid healing. You can also do this with a pair of crystals. Use one crystal to draw out the pain or disease and use another crystal to send positive healing energy to the area afflicted.

Carry a crystal in your pocket to help with courage, stress or anxiety. Pop a small crystal in your purse to bring money your way. Have crystals set out around the house to soak up any negative energy and to send out positive vibes. If you are having trouble sleeping, put a crystal under your pillow to aid peaceful sleep. Give a child a crystal to carry with them on their first day of school to take away nerves.

Don't worry if a crystal goes missing. In my experience sometimes crystals decide that they are needed elsewhere and will get themselves lost, only to be found by someone else who is in need of their particular abilities.

Crystal meditation

One of the exercises I like to do with crystals, especially when I receive a new one, is to do a crystal meditation. It helps me to connect with the particular crystal's energy and really understand its properties. This exercise works particularly well with quartz points or crystal clusters.

Make yourself comfortable, you can sit quietly or have gentle music or drumming on in the background, whatever suits you.

Hold the crystal in your hands in front of you. Focus on your breathing, deep breaths in… deep breaths out…

When you feel ready, gaze at and into the crystal, turn it over in your hands, and really look at it and all its details. Take your time with this step, examining it very carefully.

Then visualise yourself growing smaller or the crystal growing larger, whichever suits you, so that you can imagine yourself climbing onto and over the crystal itself.

Explore the crystal now, climbing up any points it has. If it has inclusions or cracks, visualise them as doorways, portals into the inside of the crystal. Put out your hands and feel the 'walls' of the crystal.

Notice how you feel exploring the crystal. Is it cold? Is it warm? What energies do you pick up from it?

Once you have finished your explorations climb out and return to normal size, focus once more on your breathing and slowly return to consciousness.

Make a note of what feelings and energies you found within that crystal to refer back to.

Cleansing and charging crystals

It is good practice to cleanse your crystals every once in a while, especially after you have used them for healing or spell work. Moon light is excellent for cleansing and recharging most of your stones. Sunlight is also good too. Most stones can be put under running water, but be careful that they aren't porous as this could damage them. Crystals can also be passed through incense smoke to purify them. Visualisation is also a good tool to use when cleansing and purifying crystals, envisage a bright white light cleansing and clearing the stone.

Crystal properties

Here is a basic chart of intents and the crystals that have those properties, but I urge you to work with crystals you believe are the right ones to use for your purpose.

Astral projection: quartz, opal

Business success: bloodstone, malachite, green tourmaline

Courage: agate, amethyst, bloodstone, carnelian, lapis lazuli, tiger's eye, turquoise

Dreams: amethyst, azurite

Friendship: chrysophrase, pink tourmaline, turquoise

Grounding: hematite, moonstone, obsidian, black tourmaline

Happiness: amethyst, chrysophrase

Healing: agate, amber, amethyst, bloodstone, calcite, carnelian, chrysophrase, quartz, garnet, hematite, hag stones, jasper, jet, lapis lazuli, sodalite, sugilite, turquoise

Love: amber, beryl, calcite, chrysocolla, emerald, jade, lapis lazuli, lepidolite, moonstone, pearl, sapphire, topaz, pink tourmaline, turquoise

Luck: apache tear, aventurine, chalcedony, chrysophrase, opal, pearl, tiger's eye, turquoise

Meditation: geodes, sapphire, sodalite

Money and prosperity: aventurine, bloodstone, calcite, emerald, jade, opal, pearl, peridot, sapphire, tiger's eye, topaz, green tourmaline

Peace: amethyst, aquamarine, aventurine, calcite, carnelian, lepidolite, obsidian, rhodocrosite, blue tourmaline

Protection: agate, amber, apache tear, calcite, carnelian, chalcedony, chrysophrase, citrine, quartz, fossils, garnet, hag stones, jade, jasper, jet, lapis lazuli, lepidolite, malachite, moonstone, obsidian, petrified wood, serpentine, sunstone, tiger's eye, black tourmaline

Psychic powers: amethyst, azurite, beryl, citrine, quartz, hag stones, lapis lazuli

Sleep: moonstone, peridot, blue tourmaline

Success: amazonite, chrysophrase

Wisdom: chrysocolla, coral, jade, sodalite, sugilite

Chapter 25

Herbs

I have a small town garden but it is big enough to house some decent size shrubs. I have a lovely big camellia that I save all the fallen flowers from to use in prosperity spells and two honeysuckle plants, again that I save the flowers from – along with several rose bushes. Rose petals can be dried and used for all sorts of magical workings and are lovely to scatter when casting a circle in ritual.

I also have lots of herbs in pots. Even if you don't have a garden try to keep a couple of flower pots with herbs in on a windowsill, they are so useful.

Mother Nature provides us with a huge host of medicinal and magical plants, pretty much every plant in the wild or in your garden has magical properties. A lot of them have medicinal uses too (not all and please, please double check before ingesting any plants as some of them might be poisonous!).

Let's go over some basics of herbalism first.

Only buy or harvest what you need

If you are gathering your herbs in the wild or from your garden, only take what you need, leave enough on the plant for it to survive. Herbs do not keep forever so don't have huge stocks, even dried herbs don't last indefinitely.

Storage

If you are drying your own herbs, or if you have purchased them dried, keep them in a cool place out of sunlight. Dark glass jars are the best form of storage vessel. If you dry your own herbs, make sure you do so correctly so that they don't rot and make sure they are properly labelled with the plant name and date you collected them.

From the wild

If you do forage in the wild, please, please make sure you can correctly identify the plant that you are harvesting or the results could be disastrous. Please also make sure that the plant you are intending to harvest from is not protected or endangered. Do make sure you only take a little of the plant and leave enough for it to survive properly. Make sure the plant is not near any fields that have been sprayed with pesticide or near car fumes.

Ingesting

I can't reiterate this enough, if you are intending to ingest the herb or plant you have collected please make sure you have identified it correctly and that it is not harmful in any way.

Safety

Do not give herbal mixtures to pregnant women, babies or young children unless you are 100 per cent sure it is safe for them to use.

Herbs are considered to be safe because they are natural. However, while they are safer than many chemical medicines, this is only true if they are used properly. Inappropriate use of some herbs could be dangerous; this includes combining them with prescription medicines or using them to treat a serious illness without consulting a doctor. Some may not be used in pregnancy, some herbs cannot be used in combination with aspirin or other remedies, and some herbs irritate the stomach. Some herbs should not be used for children (under 11 years of age).

Illness

If the illness you are intending to treat with herbal remedies is major, please get a professional diagnosis and let your practitioner know what remedies you intend to take. Some herbal remedies can react badly with modern medicines.

Cleanliness

When preparing herbal remedies, it is vital to keep everything spotless; your work surfaces, jars you keep the herbs in, your hands, any utensils you use.

If you are intending to make and use herbal remedies it is advisable to have a basic understanding of the human body and how it works. This will enable you to distinguish symptoms common to an illness and to know when to refer to a qualified medical herbalist or conventional practitioner.

Magical herbs

Every herb, plant, tree and flower has magical properties. They will also be aligned to one of the elements too.

You can use herbs as part of your spell work.

Candle spells

Crush dried herbs and spices, dress the candle with a little oil and then roll the candle in the herbs. Or as you light the candle sprinkle some of the herbs over the top.

Poppets

Use herbs and spices to stuff inside poppets (see Chapter 40).

Medicine bags

Add herbs and spices to your medicine bag, or crush them finely and use them to 'feed' the bags.

Incense

Herbs, plants and spices can all be used as ingredients in incense or burnt on their own for their scent or for their magical properties.

Offerings and other uses

Use crushed herbs as offerings to deity. Herbs can also be used in witch's bottles and magic powders. The list of uses for magical herbs is endless really.

Enchanting herbs for spell work

Before you use herbs in any spell work you will need to enchant them, to charge them with your intent and increase their effectiveness. You should charge the herbs just before you are about to use them to make sure the energy is fresh and at its strongest.

If you are using more than one herb in a spell you can charge all the herbs together or do them individually, the choice is yours.

How to enchant herbs

Hold the herb in your hand, or put it in a clean bowl and hold the bowl in both your hands. Calm and centre yourself and then reach out with your senses to pick up the vibrations of the herb, then place your power hand either just over the herb or touching it. Visualise your intent and then send this energy into the herb. You can also say a chant at this point too if you wish.

Some common herbs and their magical uses:

Lemon balm: love, success, healing
Basil: love, exorcism, wealth, flying, protection
Bay: protection, psychic powers, healing, purification, strength
Birch: protection, exorcism, purification
Camellia: riches
Carnation: protection, strength, healing
Cinnamon: spirituality, success, healing, power, psychic powers, lust, protection, love
Dandelion: divination, wishes, calling spirits
Fennel: protection, healing, purification
Ivy: protection, healing
Lavender: love, protection, sleep, chastity, longevity, purification,

happiness, peace

Marjoram: protection, love, happiness, health, money

Mint: money, lust, healing, travel, exorcism, protection

Nettle: exorcism, protection, healing, lust

Parsley: lust, protection, purification

Poppy: fertility, love, sleep, money, luck, invisibility

Rose: love, psychic powers, healing, love divination, luck, protection

Rosemary: protection, love, lust, mental powers, exorcism, purification, healing, sleep

Sage: immortality, wishes, longevity, wisdom, protection

Harvesting and drying your own herbs

The best time to harvest an herb depends on the type of herb. Most need to be harvested just as the flower buds appear. The summer and autumn are the best times of the year.

Early morning is the best time of day to harvest herbs just after the sun has dried the leaves but before it gets too hot.

Annual herbs can be harvested heavily, cut back just above a pair of leaves or a leaf, leaving 4in to 6in of stem. If it's the seeds you require, don't cut it back at all. Leave it to flower and harvest once the seed heads are turning brown.

Perennial herbs should only have one third of the top growth harvested and sometimes just the tips of the leaves.

To harvest herbs, the tools I use are a pair of pruners or a sharp pair of scissors, but a sharp knife could be used as well.

To dry bunches of herbs, wash them and dry them, then tie the stems in a bundle and hang upside down in a warm dark place (you can cover them in a brown bag). Leave them for about two to four weeks. I use this method for herbs such as rosemary and bay; it works best with herbs that don't have high moisture content.

For individual leaves or smaller herbs, lay them on a tray and keep them in a warm dark place. I use this method for rose petals or sometimes for small stems of thyme.

If you need herbs to be dried quicker put them in an oven on a baking tray at around 180 degrees Fahrenheit for three to four hours. Or use the microwave, putting the clean herbs on a kitchen towel for one to three minutes, turning them over every 30 seconds.

To store dried herbs, I prefer to use dark brown glass jars with airtight lids. Keeping the light out extends the life of them.

Herbal tea

This is one of the easiest ways to make an herbal remedy. You use the leaves and/or the flowers of a plant for tea. Use a glass or ceramic pot or cup to infuse the herb. Use one or two teaspoons of the herb, pour on hot water and brew for at least five minutes, then strain. You can drink it warm or chill it and drink it with ice. It can also be used as a mouthwash, gargle or hair rinse. (Only keep for a maximum of 24 hours).

Decoction

This is a good way to use plant bark, berries and roots. Chop fresh or dried herbs and simmer them in water for about 20 minutes. Strain them and then drink. This can also be used as a mouthwash or gargle. (Only keep for a maximum of 48 hours). Use one heaped teaspoon of chopped herb material to one and a half cups (12 ½ fl oz) of water.

Tincture

Tinctures are made by macerating (which means soaking) chopped herbs from any part of the plant in an alcohol solution. Sometimes vinegar or glycerol is used instead of alcohol. The ratio of herb to water and alcohol will determine the strength of the tincture, but the most common ratio is one part herb to three parts water and alcohol. The proportion of alcohol varies from 25 per cent to 90 per cent. Tinctures do have a long shelf life, but usually take at least a week to prepare. Place the chopped herb material in a clean, preferably sterilised jar and stir in the required amount of alcohol. For each 4oz of dried herb material add half pint of alcohol solution. Stir, then close with a lid, leave for 10 days. Make sure to shake the jar every day. After 10 days strain and put into a clean bottle. Vodka is the preferred alcohol to use, but I have successfully used whisky too. Fresh plant material needs a 40 per cent alcohol solution. Dried plant material can be made with 25 per cent alcohol. If it is below 25 per cent the tincture may decay.

Other ways of storing herbs

To freeze herbs, wash and blanch them then drop them into ice water and place in bags or ice cube trays, then freeze. This works well with moisture-dense herbs such as basil, chives and parsley.

To make an herb vinegar, cover the herbs in white vinegar and steep for four to six weeks in bottles.

For herb butter add four tablespoons of dried herbs and a squeeze of lemon juice to ½lb of softened butter.

For herb mustard, mix 1tbs of dry mustard, the same of salt and a tsp of sugar, mix to a paste with vinegar, split into four and mix with 1tbs of herbs.

Herbs also work well in pot pourri – start with a base of rose petals and lavender then add whatever dried herbs you like, add whole cloves or cinnamon. Add benzoin to fix, then store in an air-tight jar for four to five weeks. Then it's ready.

You can also make lavender sugar – add dried lavender heads to a jar of sugar. It's wonderful to use in cookie or cake recipes. You can also use the stems of lavender on the fire to make your home smell sweet.

Hot infused oil is only used externally. You need to put your fresh herbs in a jar and cover with oil – olive, almond or sunflower. Put the jar in a saucepan of water up to its neck and bring the water to a simmer for three hours. Then strain into a brown glass bottle.

Cold infused oils are made in a similar way, but instead of heating in a saucepan of water you put the jar on a sunny windowsill instead.

An ointment covers and protects the skin; a good base for an ointment is petroleum jelly. The jelly is melted in a double boiler and herbs are added, simmered until they are crisp and strained into jars.

A cream is made from oil, beeswax and water and this penetrates the skin. Melt 1oz beeswax in a double boiler; add one cup (8 fl oz) of olive oil and mix. Add 2oz of your chosen herb. (If it's too thick add a small amount of water and mix). Simmer for 20 minutes, stirring. Add a drop of benzoin to preserve. Then strain into sterilized jars.

Common herbs and their medicinal properties

Mint: antiseptic, antispasmodic, diaphoretic, mild analgesic, mild bitter, mild sedative, relives wind

Lemon balm: antidepressant, antispasmodic, insect repellent, relaxant, relieves wind, topical anti viral

Cinnamon: antimicrobial, aromatic, astringent, mild stimulant, relieves wind

Meadowsweet: antacid, anti inflammatory, anti rheumatic, astringent

Rosemary: anti inflammatory, antioxidant, antispasmodic, circulatory stimulant, digestive tonic, nerve tonic

Sage: antimicrobial, antioxidant, astringent, digestive tonic, oestrogenic, general tonic, reduces sweating

Chickweed: astringent, cooling (topically), demulcent, relieves itchiness

Dandelion: bitter tonic, diuretic, liver cleanser, mild laxative

Cayenne pepper: antiseptic, counter irritant, local analgesic, relieves wind and spasms, stimulant, tonic

Hawthorn: antioxidant, heart tonic, lowers blood pressure, relaxes blood vessels

Chapter 26

Trees

Trees have a huge amount of power, energy and magic within them and this can be utilised in meditation, spell work and magical tools.

Hug a tree – no it's not just for old hippies! Next time you are out and about find yourself a tree, walk slowly up to it and in your mind ask permission to make contact. Usually you will get a good feeling or even a mental 'yes' in your head. On the odd occasion you will get an uncomfortable feeling or a definite 'no' response, on those rare occasions thank the tree and walk away. But, if you get a good vibe, slowly raise both hands on either side of the trunk of the tree and see if you can make contact with the energy field surrounding the tree. You should start to feel a light resistance a few inches out from the trunk, then you can slowly move your hands to touch the tree itself. Take a few moments to connect with the spirit of the tree, called a dryad. Sense the energy, notice whether you detect it as a cold or warm energy, and see what messages or feelings you get. When you are ready, thank the tree and if possible leave a small offering (biodegradable please). Try this exercise with different types of tree; you should notice that they all have their very own unique energy patterns.

Tree meditation

Use this base meditation but meet a different tree each time, using the tree correspondences below.

Sit comfortably and focus on your breathing to start meditating.

As the familiar world around you dissipates, you find yourself on a pathway. It winds and twists off into the distance. You start to follow the path, with each step going deeper into the meditation.

As you walk, notice the scenery around you, the sky, the grass, fields, and mountains – what do you see?

The pathway leads you to a small copse of trees. You can hear the noise of the leaves as the breeze makes them sing; you hear birds singing and smell the fresh air.

You enter the copse and right in the centre is a lone tree, standing as if it has been waiting for your arrival, you walk slowly towards it, noticing all the details – the colour and texture of the bark, the colour and shape of the leaves and the height of it.

Once you reach the tree, put your hand out and touch the bark, notice how it feels under your finger tips. Reach up and place your other hand on the trunk as well. Ask the tree if you may connect with the energy. Feel the connection taking hold, notice the type of energy. Feel the power and strength of the tree's spirit.

Feel the energy flowing from the tree, through your palms, down your arms, radiating through your body and then down through your legs and out through the soles of your feet and into the Earth.

Ask the tree if it has any messages or wisdom for you.

When you are ready, thank the tree for its energy and wisdom and slowly remove your hands.

Turn and make your way back out of the copse, then back down the pathway, still taking in the scenery around you.

Once you reach the spot where you began, slowly come back to your reality.

Wriggling your fingers and toes, open your eyes.

Don't forget to ground when you have finished meditating.

Tree correspondences

This is a basic list, but as I always say (are you bored with me saying it yet?) go with your instincts, listen to your intuition and go with what you believe the correspondences for each tree are.

Birch: new beginnings, changes, cleansing, birth, letting go of unwanted emotions and habits, new growth, new directions and inspirations

Elder: generosity, renewal, regeneration, the cycle of death and rebirth, transformation and understanding

Rowan: spiritual strength, psychic abilities, intuition, protection, vitality, life affirming, energy work, creativity, possibilities and inner strength

Hazel: wisdom, knowledge, creativity, inspiration, friendships, inner wisdom, ideas, flexibility and solutions

Ash: existence, understanding, perspective, ancient wisdom, inner wisdom, dreams, visions, intuition, perspective, universal understanding, connectivity, actions and reactions

Yew: death and rebirth, transformation, ancestors, our past, life cycles, Otherworld and transformation. (The wood and the bark of the Yew tree are poisonous so please be careful not to inhale any dust if you are sanding or cutting this wood. Most parts of the Yew are poisonous to ingest.)

Holly: balance, direction, love, emotions, communication, feelings, life force and energy

Willow: intuition, unconscious, inspiration, fertility, dreams, visions, inner strength, healing, flexibility, direction, emotions and female energy

Alder: perspective, balance, protection, challenges, foundations, stability, balance, instincts, faeries and the Otherworld

Hawthorn: love, fertility, protection, matters of the heart, energy release, spiritual growth, faeries, meditation, possibilities, potential and good fortune

Oak: courage, inner strength, doorway to the Otherworld, endurance, self determination, durability, power, dealing with challenges and inner guidance

Apple: abundance, generosity, cleansing, gratitude, trust and love

Blackthorn: challenge, perspective, outlook, choices and intuition

Pine: prosperity, purification, endurance, fertility, alleviating guilt, warding against negativity and illness

Chapter 27

Animal Totems and Guides

I work with animal totems and guides a lot. Some have come to me via meditations, and some have come to me purely by the fact that I keep seeing them, they keep leaving me feathers or people keep mentioning them to me.

My lifelong totem is Wild Boar. He has been with me for several years now and came to me in a meditation designed by a friend to connect me with the male aspect of deity. The meditation worked to do just that, but also brought Boar to me. He is with me all the time lending his particular energies, strength, support and wisdom.

I also work with the energy of Unicorn as well on and off when I need the energies Unicorn offers.

Other totems that I work with on a regular basis are Magpie, Pigeon and Seagull. I know when I need to 'borrow' their particular wisdom or characteristics because they leave me feathers or visit my garden and 'shout' at me. When I travel on Otherworld journeys it is Panther that accompanies me, he is my strong and silent guide then.

Animal magic shows you how to work with animals for your spiritual growth and increased magical power.

Your work with your familiar/totem/guides can take on an even greater purpose that is the remembrance and honouring of our ancestors. You can use familiars/totems/guides in meditations and magic. Use chants to invoke an animal's greatest natural attribute. You can discover a new source of strength, wisdom and friendship.

The word familiar in the dictionary is defined as:

Closely acquainted; an intimate associate or companion; a spirit often embodied in an animal and held to attend and serve or guard a person.

To most people a familiar is a witch's companion, a small animal that helps the witch with magic.

You may already have an actual physical familiar living in your home in the guise of a pet. Do you find yourself receiving mental messages from your familiar? This type of communication is common between people and their pet/familiar.

You may even have an astral bodied animal familiar, drawn to you by your enthusiasm for that particular creature with which it is impossible to have contact in the physical realm. Many people collect pictures or statues of a particular creature and never consciously realise they are subconsciously communicating with that creature.

What is the difference between an animal totem, a familiar and an animal spirit guide?

Totems are those animals that you have had an affinity with or which seem to have walked with you for a very long time period. They may have walked with you for many lifetimes, many years, or just recently came into focus as you have had need of them. Your totem animal need not be limited to animals on this planet at this time; mythical creatures and extinct ones are useful totems too.

A familiar is a magical working companion, a creature that lends its energies to yours for protection, meditational guidance, inspiration, and spell casting as well as for better understanding of and communication with a particular species.

Guides are animals that come around quickly as you need help at certain times of your life and then just as quickly leave. They may linger as long as a glance or for many months. Distinguishing guides from totems can be difficult but not impossible. If you are needing help at the moment in your life or something happens, then the animal that has crossed your path more than likely was a guide giving you wisdom to help you along the way. You don't choose a spirit guide, it chooses you.

Then there is animal medicine. The term medicine refers to the special powers housed in each part of creation, including the animal kingdom. By observing animals in natural surroundings and their associated behaviours, we begin to get glimpses of each creature's medicine. This understanding in turn helps us to connect with the animal spirit, honour it and utilize it in our witchery.

How to find your familiar or totem animal

There are meditations, dreams, dancing, drumming, spells or just being particularly drawn to one animal or seeing images of it in everyday life.

Once you find your animal you need to research it. Work to understand it. Where does it live? What does it eat? How does it act, walk, hunt, and look after its young? You can expand that to cover what element it corresponds to. How does it defend itself? Does it have its own legends or folklore? All these things will help you to understand your animal more and learn why it found you. Remember that there will be positive AND negative characteristics to any animal.

What about shapeshifting?

Shapeshifting is a change, a way to help us become better by becoming different than ourselves. We already shapeshift every day in many different ways to everyone we meet. We are a different person to our boss, a stranger, a spouse, our child. Native Americans shapeshifted to go on spiritual quests to learn answers about themselves and the world around them. So we may learn too to shapeshift to seek higher wisdom and knowledge.

Shapeshifting brings us closer to our totems.

So you have a totem or an animal spirit guide – but what does it mean?

Each totem or spirit guide will be with you for a reason, what you need to work out and understand is why it is with you.

Say a butterfly totem came to you – the butterfly symbolises reincarnation, magic, beauty and love. It represents transformation of the personality and life. It can also bring understanding of where you are in the cycle of your life. Using it to help with divination concerning future events that have a bearing on your cycle of life and rebirth. Relate that to your own life and situation and learn from it. The butterfly is with you to help you, assist you and guide you.

Or maybe a griffin has joined you – seeing a griffin is a sign of powerful new beginnings and of learning how to use psychic powers in a useful manner. But on the negative side it is subconscious punishment for love of riches, greed or of desiring riches. Its magical attributes are understanding the relationship between psychic energy and cosmic forces; spiritual wisdom and enlightenment. It is about bringing the dark side of ourselves into submission.

What about an otter? His magical attributes are finding inner treasures or talents; faithfulness; gaining wisdom; the ability to recover from a crisis. Be sensible, but not overly suspicious, when something or someone new enters your life. Its appearance points to a need to enjoy life rather than just endure it. It represents social life, friends, happiness and guidance to uncovering talents, psychic or physical.

But what if you want to work with a particular animal's medicine? Or think that one of them might be able to assist with a goal?

Do a spell – using a particular animal and its talents. We all go through bad times and find ourselves in situations where we feel there is no light in our lives. Do a little work with the familiar that knows all about darkness. Ask the mole to guide you forth from the underground and up into the light.

What if you performed a spell and it didn't quite work out how you expected it and you now regret it? Use the power of the chaos dragon to reverse your spell.

Need some healing for yourself or someone else? Try a healing ritual using the power of the dolphin.

All the animals have their own unique powers and can all be utilized and called upon to assist us when we need them.

So, once you have your totem animal, familiar and/or spirit guides is that it?

Nope! Everything that is worth having takes a bit of work to keep. You need to honour your guides and make sure you stay connected with them. Apart from learning all about them as I mentioned before, you do need to reaffirm your connection regularly. Make pictures of them, even if your art isn't that good. Donate to wildlife charities if you have some spare cash, even small change will help. Make charms and amulets for your familiars and pets collars. Don't ignore your spirit guides in your daily life. Take them out with you when you go anywhere, say good morning to a picture of your animal each day, put a statue on your altar, and wear a pendant representing your particular animal.

In order to form a strong bond with your guide, familiar or totem animal, mutual respect is essential. You must listen to your guide's point of view and suggestions.

Working with animal magic takes time and effort, but can be very rewarding and enlightening.

A meditation to meet an animal guide or messenger

Take several deep breaths in and out...

As your room around you dissipates you find yourself in a large cave. There are natural handmade rugs on the floor and rough paintings on the cave walls.

There is a fire in the centre with a pot hanging over it, and various herbs and flowers hanging from the roof to dry. You can smell musky and aromatic scents.

Behind you, you can hear water, as you turn you see that the side of the cave is open to the sky. It is night time and dark, but the whole sky is scattered with beautiful stars.

You make your way to the edge and realise you are on a ledge, high above the sea. Waves are crashing onto the rocks below, and rainbows are thrown up along with the waves.

You notice a path curving downwards through the rock. You start to follow this path downwards, the waves crashing onto the rocks beside you. You can feel the vibrations and power of the water and can smell and taste the salt, feeling the fine mist on your skin.

As you reach the bottom of the path you step out onto the shore. It is more peaceful here, calm and relaxing.

As you adjust to your surroundings you notice that behind you now is a forest of beautiful old trees, with a blanket of wild herbs beneath their feet. Listen to the leaves rustling in the trees. Smell the scent of the wild herbs that the air brings to you. In amongst the herbs are strands of washed up seaweed, shells, pebbles and twigs.

You wander along the boundary, looking at the ocean on one side, the trees on the other. Take note of the leaves, the branches, the shells, and the herbs – all that you see around you.

You notice a large, flat rock just on the boundary between the sea and the forest. You make your way to it and sit down. Behind you are the sounds of the forest; in front of you is the ocean. The waves have a rhythmic, soothing sound, like the slow beating of a drum.

Let your thoughts drift just for a moment and take in the sounds of the sea, the sounds of the forest and the scent of sea air, and wild herbs. Take it all in.

Movement appears in the corner of your vision, you turn and look – it may have come from the sea, it may have come from the beach, it may have come from the forest or even from the sky…

It is a creature…

As it comes closer, you can make out what creature it is, its colour and its markings. This is an animal spirit guide. One that is meant for you. It has a message for you. You listen…

When you have listened to its message the creature indicates that you are to follow it back up the pathway to the cave. You stand and then follow it back along the beach to the base of the cliff. It leads you up the narrow pathway to the ledge of the cave.

There is a choice now, this animal guide may come with you, or it may turn and depart.

If it stays it is a totem guide and will be with you for as long as you need it. Even if you forget it is there or withdraw from it, it will still walk in the shadows guiding and guarding you. If the animal turns and departs then it was a spirit messenger, take note of the message it gave you.

The cave dissipates and your room reappears around you.

Stretch your arms and come back into focus, opening your eyes.

Totem correspondences

Here is a basic list of animals and their energies, but go with what you feel.

Ant: teamwork, patience, being at one with yourself, hard working

Badger: aggression, self expression, reliance, holding your own, the underworld

Bat: avoiding obstacles, barriers, transformation, releasing, illusion, rebirth, dreams

Bear: inner knowledge, healing, strength, stamina, balance, harmony, astral travel

Bees: concentration, prosperity, reincarnation, awakening, industriousness, dreams

Boar: self reliance, protection, spiritual and warrior strength, personal power

Butterfly: change, creativity, freedom, joy, the soul, transformation, courage

Cat: independence, flexibility, agility, telepathic abilities, healing, curiosity, magic

Crow: change, messages, intelligence, communication, mystery, illusion, omens

Deer/stag: grace, gentleness, alertness, hunting, seeking, intuition, transformation

Dog: loyalty, faithfulness, communication, love, teamwork, hard work, dedication

Dolphins: healing, emotions, intuition, psychic abilities, wisdom, freedom, trust

Dragonfly: change, illusions, dreams, truth, wisdom, enlightenment

Eagle: strength, courage, wisdom, keen sight, knowledge, magic, spiritual truth

Fish: abundance, prosperity, children, harmony, divination, prophecy

Fox: cleverness, cunning, camouflage, persistence, wisdom, reliable friend

Frog/toad: patience, transformation, sexual energy, lust, resurrection, luck

Goat: abundance, independence, energy of nature, agility, instinct

Hawk: observation, memory, past lives, omens, dreams, overcoming problems

Horse: stamina, endurance, faithfulness, freedom, friendship, travel

Ladybird (bug): past lives, enlightenment, renewal, protection, luck, wishes

Lion: relaxation, releasing stress and tension, family, strength, courage, energy

Magpie: intelligence, the occult, jack of all trades, perceptive, social, wilful

Owl: keen sight, unmasking, wisdom, magic, freedom, clairvoyance, messages

Panther: cunning, strength, perseverance, boldness, astral travel, the Otherworld

Peacock: dignity, self confidence, divination

Rabbit/hare: transformation, hidden teachings, quick thinking, intuition

Raven: introspection, courage, magic, healing, secrets, mysticism, rebirth

Robin: happiness, new beginnings, guidance, growth, renewal

Shark: survival, adaptability, independence, power, balance, fearlessness

Snake: creativity, wisdom, understanding, spirit, facing your fears, initiations

Spider: wisdom, creativity, inspiration, new projects, balance, weaver of fate

Swan: dreams, transitions, spiritual evolution, intuition, divination

Whale: wisdom, intuition, connection, psychic abilities, inner depth

Wolf: individuality, loyalty, spirituality, teacher, pathfinder

Don't forget the mythical totem creatures too:

Unicorn: purity, innocence, magic, enchantment, faeries, valour, morality

Phoenix: rebirth, renewal, spiritual growth, energy

Griffin: understanding, spiritual wisdom, enlightenment, balance, vigilance

Centaur: healing, divination, the arts, inspiration, impulses, emotions

I have been asked if someone could have something like a

dinosaur as a totem and I answered honestly 'why not?' If an animal comes to you in spirit with wisdom, strength or just a message then don't ignore it, no matter how strange or silly you might think it is, that spirit animal came to you for a reason. I have found it is always wise to listen...

Chapter 28

Dragons

Dragon magic is an ancient and fascinating subject and one that covers so much that there are many entire books on it. Hopefully what I have tried to do here is cover the basics and maybe whet your appetite just a little.

There are different views of what dragons are and of what they represent. They are sometimes viewed as mythological entities which represent a set of principles.

A dragon viewed as a winged serpent could be a symbol of the Earth and the underworld. The wings can be seen as a symbol of the heavens. The winged serpent brings together these two principles – as above, so below.

The Chinese dragon is a symbol of Tao, that which is beyond all terms and all polarities but also the force behind all (Yin and Yang).

The dragon represents the unknown, the hidden energy in humans and in nature.

The word dragon comes from the Greek verb 'derkein' which means 'to see'. The dragon is the principle of clear seeing: the ability to see things in a new light as they really are, beyond all illusions.

You might be familiar with the idea of a dragon hoarding his treasure. It is that treasure that symbolises the wisdom it keeps. For us to find the knowledge it guards we must quest for it within ourselves and venture into the unknown to find the answers.

If you have ever practised yoga you will know the dragon as the kundalini, the force that is hidden inside us.

We all have it within us to awaken the forces within the dragon.

The world of dragons includes many different breeds, types, colours, sizes and shapes. Some you may be more familiar with than others – the Chinese or the Welsh dragon for instance – others such as the Worm of Wyrd may be new to you. But no matter what they look like, they all hold incredible power.

A dragon can be a strong, useful and wise totem or guardian and we can also tap into dragon energy to use within our rituals and our magic.

Dragons are a primeval force, they are physical and spiritual, they bring with them the full force and power of the elements. They are also very wise and intelligent.

By now you should be very used to using energy and maybe even sensing energy fields. If you pick up the feeling of a large energy field around you then chances are it is a dragon.

Whether dragons did used to roam the earth I don't know, I like to think so. But now they exist in the astral and spiritual planes.

Dragon energy is one of the most powerful energies I know of and when blended together via the four main elements, creates the etheric dragon… a super power.

Dragon energy is linear, so be careful what you ask for. You will receive it in the most direct way possible. Be very specific about your intentions, integrity and intelligence. Dragons do not necessarily use human logic; if you offer them a problem they will find a solution, but it will be a straightforward one, removing anything in its path to solve it…

Dragon energy is very good at removing dark energy. It is good for clearing negative energy, but make sure you also ask for positive energy to be left in its place. And I have found it is always best to end your request with 'and do no harm'. Dragon magic works quickly and can sometimes have unexpected results.

As witches usually have an element we favour to work with so do dragons. Not everyone believes that we have 'elemental dragons' as such, they aren't necessarily made up from one particular element, just that they work best with one element, although you will also find a few that work well with all the elements, these are particularly powerful.

While I don't want to put you off working with dragons, I would ask you to remember that these are very old and very wise creatures. They also have a tendency to get bored easily and are impatient! So always treat them with the respect that you would a wise elder.

What I can tell you is that working with dragon energy can be very beneficial and a wonderful experience. Dragons also have so much to teach us, all that ancient wisdom waiting to be shared with us not to mention all their powerful energy and support that they can provide us with.

And a word about the chaos dragon, usually dark purple in colour the chaos dragon is really a bit of a mischief maker! Just keep an eye on him and you will be fine. He is, however, extremely useful to call upon when you need to undo a spell.

Dragon lines

You will all have probably heard the term 'ley lines' before, magnetic fields of energy that form lines crossing and intersecting over the Earth.

Centuries ago the Chinese called ley lines 'dragon lines'. When the dragon lines cross each other their energy spirals and becomes a vortex. If several lines cross at a certain point (a node) it can produce a huge vortex of energy. Avebury in the UK has 12 lines that meet and go down into the Earth; this is where the stones are placed.

Healing

Dragon energy is very useful for healing; you can channel it when using crystal healing or in hands-on healing, but there is also a form of Reiki that combines dragon energy too for the purpose of healing.

In ritual

You can call upon dragons in your quarter calls, as you would call in the elements.

Dragon totem/guardian

Having a dragon totem is very special; they are incredibly powerful and wise.

I have always had a connection with dragons, I was drawn to stories and images of them as a child and that connection has followed me through to adulthood.

I have one large red fire dragon totem. He doesn't appear very often and if he does it is usually because I have refused to listen or am being particularly stubborn about something to do with my own health or wellbeing. I find myself standing in a dark shadow as he looms up behind me, not that I ever turn around, but if I did I can image he would be standing there on his hind legs with his front legs crossed, the talons on his hind leg tapping impatiently on the floor and a look in his eye that says, 'You are in serious trouble, do something to sort it out now!' I also have one smaller guardian dragon, he is pale blue in colour not quite a water dragon, not quite an ice dragon, but he came to me at Stonehenge a while back when I needed some emotional healing. He appears now and then when my emotions need sorting out.

If Dragon appears as your totem it usually means you need one or some of its qualities such as strength or courage. Dragon also brings the message of balance and asks us to use our psychic abilities to see the world as magical.

Once Dragon has come to you, I do encourage you to connect with it on a regular basis, make a connection and keep it, Dragon is very useful not only as a powerful guardian but also as a guide – keep it happy!

There are many ways to strengthen your bond with your

Dragon totem. Here are a few suggestions:

Meditate upon your Dragon totem.
Collect dragon images – statues, pendants or pictures.
Read everything you can on dragons, this will not only strengthen your connection but expand your knowledge too.

Dragon totem possesses the following energies: leadership, magical prowess, vitality, mastery, insight, divine illumination, protection from outside evil forces from all directions, grounded energy, fulfilment of potential, inspiration, longevity, personal happiness, greatly increased riches, infinite wisdom, luminous beauty, majesty, indomitable spirit and strength, invisibility, power of transformation and metaphysical knowledge.

In Celtic tradition

The fire dragon is a symbol of transmutation, energy and mastery, if this is your power animal you will be lent enthusiasm, courage and vitality. Your inner fire will be fuelled. You will be helped to overcome obstacles. You will be given the qualities of leadership and mastery. The fire dragon can also be a strong protector.

The air dragon brings insight, inspiration and vitality. This power animal must be handled with the greatest of respect. With this power animal, large flashes of illumination in intellect and psyche are possible. Insight and clarity will be given for all problems. As always – trust your inner voice.

The earth dragon brings potential, power and riches. You will be shown your potential and your riches – what you are capable of. With the earth dragon's assistance, you may discover the beauty and power that lies within you, within us all. The earth dragon resides deep within the Earth and can aid you in grounding scattered energies. When you call on him for help, think of a slowly paced heavy dragon pulling himself toward you. Feel his weight surrounding you. He will nurture you like Mother Earth does.

The water dragon brings connection, depth and passion. The water dragon as a power animal brings memories and wishes, perhaps long forgotten yet hidden, to the fore. By squaring up with painful past experiences, a sense of peace and balance can be achieved in our lives. The water dragon will give you the courage and compassion in this challenge.

Each of the four elemental dragons – earth, air, water, and fire – represent power and energy. Each dragon mediates this power or energy in a different way and we must learn how to weave all four dragon energies into our being, the key being balance.

Dragon meditation

Make yourself comfortable in a place where you won't be disturbed. Close your eyes and focus on your breathing.

Your world around you dissipates and you find yourself in a clearing, In the distance you can see mountains and what looks like a volcano top with smoke creeping out of its crater. Behind you is a large dense forest and to one side you turn to see a large lake.

Look up towards the sky and see the storm clouds rolling in from over the mountain tops, although the sun is still trying to break through and long shafts of light beam down on the surface of the lake making it glint and sparkle.

You realise you are not alone. Flying high above you are shapes that look like large birds, on a second look you realise they are dragons, dark shapes weaving in and out of the clouds.

Then you hear crashing sounds coming from the forest and realise that behind the trees large dragons are moving around. But you don't feel afraid.

Splashing from the lake draws your attention and you notice that some of the glints in the water are actually dragons swimming and splashing, breaking the surface of the water.

A loud roaring sound draws your attention to the mountain tops and you see that diving in and out of the volcano crater are dragons, breathing long streams of flame as they dive.

Then on the shoreline of the lake you realise what you thought were sandy rocks now are large desert dragons sunning themselves.

Stand for a moment and draw on the powers of all these different dragons. Reach out with your mind and see if one of them makes a connection with you.

If one does, ask it to join you where you are standing. Wait until it stands beside you then ask for permission to ask it some questions. If it agrees then say what you want to know.

Once you are finished, thank the dragon for its presence, guidance and wisdom and bid it farewell. It may tell you that it is your dragon guardian now and you can call upon it any time; it may not.

Know that you can always come back to the land of dragons for guidance.

Slowly bring your focus back to the present.

When you are ready to get up, shake your arms and legs and open your eyes.

Chapter 29

The World of Faerie

The word fairy or faerie comes from the ancient French faes, derived from the Latin fata. It was first used around the 13th or 14th century to describe spirit beings that had been central for hundreds of years in the oral folk tradition of many lands.

Faerie or fairy originally meant a state of enchantment or glamour, the power of illusion, reflecting the power of beings that might bring blessings or curses and ambivalence towards such beings. It was fear of angering the faery folk by speaking their name that led to their being given a variety of euphemisms that might, by a process of magic, attract only their benevolence.

What do you think of as faeries?

The general idea is to think of faeries as little flittery things with gossamer wings, stripy tights and a pink tutu. There are of course many, many races and types of faerie – as wide and diverse as human cultures, if not more so, and quite possibly none of them have ever worn a pink tutu.

Scientists remain unconvinced about the existence of such insubstantial creatures. They cannot be pinned down long enough to be measured or tested, or to answer a questionnaire on whether they prefer acorns or buttercups.

But, all the possible explanations for the existence of the fae contribute to our understanding of a spiritual force that can be sensed if not seen in places of natural beauty. It may even be that faeries are becoming more visible, as they were in pre-industrial days; because we need a reminder of the consequences of a consumer society in which instant gratification has assumed undue importance. This is the danger of being seduced by our own visions of faerie gold and glamour.

By using different faerie forms as a focus for ritual, clairvoyance and psychic development we can explore different aspects of our own nature and strengthen our connections with creatures and places as a source of personal power.

The races of faerie folk

The races and types of faerie folk include: abatwa, ballybog, bean fionn, bean nighe, bean sidhe, bean tighe, blue men of Minch, boggarts, bokwus, brownie, bwca, Cailleac, cluricaun, coblynau, corrigan, cururipur, deva, djinn, domovoi, dryad, duendes, duergar, dwarves, ekimmu, ellyllon, elves, fauns, fees, fenoderee, ferrishyn, folletti, Formorians, fossegrim, fylgiar, gans, ghillie dhu, gianes, gnomes, goblins, gremlins, gruagach, gwragedd Annwn, Gwyllion, hamadryadniks, hill trows, hobgoblins, hu hsien, hyldermoder, hyter sprites, ieles, jimaninos, kachinas, kappa, kelpies, knockers, korrs, kul, leprechauns, linchetti, lorelei, lunantishess, lutins, manitou, matka syra ziemia, mazikeen, merrows, mimis, moors, moss people, nagas, nunnehi, nymphs, pechs, penates, phookas, pixies, rozhinitsy, red caps, salamanders, satyrs, selkies, spriggans, sylphs, tengu, tokolush, tomtra, torngak, trolls, tylwyth teg, undines and yumboes.

And that's just the tip of the iceberg, there are many, many more…

What do you need in order to enter the faerie realm?

You need to believe… believe that there is more out there than that which we can normally see.

Where does the realm of faerie exist?

The faerie realm is just that, a realm in its own right that runs alongside ours and every so often our worlds intersect. Media and literature would have us imagine all sorts of wonderful, mystical, faraway places to be the land of the fae. In actual fact faerie is all around us. Nature provides us with the portals; we just need to open our inner eyes to see them.

So, you want to see or work with the fae – what do you think they need from us to enable this interaction?

The fae do like meeting with humans, but they are quite particular. The most important things to remember that the fae require are RESPECT and TRUST.

As witches we would never even contemplate destroying nature – because of who we are and what we believe, but what we also need to think about is that nature is where the fae hang out. To destroy their habitat or meeting places would not put you in their good books.

The fae are also famous for their sense of humour and their practical jokes, so you also need to be able to laugh with them.

If you are open with them, respect them and their habitats, honour them, and show them your trust, then you will be able to work with them. Most importantly NEVER COMMAND them or DEMAND anything from them. This sort of action will break all ties with them. If you would like to work with them, then invite them or request their company as you would with a special friend.

How do you go about contacting the fae?

You could request their presence while in circle, invite them to represent the four directions. Do this as you would usually call the quarters, but invite them in rather than command them.

You can also use meditation; this is an excellent way to contact the fae via the astral plane.

You could also take yourself off outside. Go and find a place in nature to sit quietly to see if you can catch a glimpse of them, the beach, a park, the garden, a forest, streams – pretty much anywhere outside where it is quiet.

Cast a spell or make a charm requesting the ability to see the fae.

Make yourself a faerie altar in your home or your garden.

This gives you a physical focus on the unseen realms in your home, your own personal portal into the realms of the fae. The altar needs to be in the north of your home if possible. This is considered the most sacred direction in faeriecraft; it is also the place through which the sun passes at night. This represents the most profound aspects of our subconscious minds, the place of magic and mystery.

Decorating possibilities for your faerie altar are endless and very personal to you.

What would you put on a faerie altar?

You could use sparkly things, tree lights, faerie ornaments, crystals, feathers, glitter. If you want to attract earthier fae you could use moss, driftwood and twigs, or perhaps a sea theme with shells and driftwood. And the fae love mirrors! The only thing not to put on your altar is metal, particularly iron as faeries have a strong aversion to it. Although silver, gold and copper are acceptable.

Use this altar as a focus, leave offerings for the fae, communicate with them here, tell them your thoughts, and express your wishes and spells. Faeries, as a quirk of their nature, dislike being thanked and displays of gratitude. They do, however, demand respect and appreciate small tokens or gifts. But of course they are particular about what gifts they like too. They love milk, cream, cake, butter and mead. Leaving some in a small shell or a walnut shell would be just right.

To request fae in circle, you could use the four elementals – gnomes for earth/north, sylphs for air/east, undines for water/west, and salamanders for fire/south. See the later chapter on elementals.

The fae can and will protect your home in as much as they are able. They can bring lightness to a home darkened by arguments, grief and personality clashes. They can lighten the atmosphere.

Healing the home and those who dwell there is not something

for which you often have to make a formal plea. House fae, like brownies, house gnomes, beantighs, faeries of the hearth and nature spirits, want the energy around your land in a positive state of balance because they live there too.

What spells do you think the fae could help with?

There are numerous spells for working with the fae, for house protection, healing illnesses, and finding lost objects. Use faerie dream magic to answer questions. Use faerie plants to heal illnesses. Use elemental faerie magic for wholeness and wellbeing. Use faerie spells to heal emotions and faerie astral projection to heal your spirituality.

Most regular adventurers in the realm of faerie are eventually given some gift, which may either help in healing or diagnosing, or by offering safe passages throughout the Otherworld. Until such a gift is presented, a simple bottle oracle known as the seguro – made with thought and care with your own hands – can fulfil this role.

Faerie seguro

The seguro is not just a diagnostic tool, it is also a spirit ally. These healing bottles are used by faerie shamans. The bottles contain specific plant or herbal totems that help the shamans focus attention on a cure for an ailment. A shaman might use one seguro for an entire lifetime, or might have several they consult depending on the situation.

Over a century ago in Ireland lived a woman named Biddy Early. This elderly rural woman was gifted with a blue glass bottle from the faeries – a seguro. When neighbours came for her healing help, she would peer into the bottle, get the right diagnosis and be told what herb, plant, tea or ritual was needed to heal those people. Her fame spread, and soon people from all over Ireland migrated to Biddy Early's door to ask for her services. As she continued to heal more and more people of diseases no doctor at that time could manage, her own health deteriorated. She was plagued with rheumatoid arthritis for the last half of her life. Today the blue bottle is said to lie at the bottom of the lake near her home. From time to time divers have searched vainly for it, but it is buried in the silt at the lake bottom, or has been reclaimed by the faeries.

Some shamans will add to a seguro over time, or they will sometimes reconstruct the seguro from the same bottle so as not to disturb the vibrations the bottle has absorbed that have worked well for so long. With use, and with each item added to the seguro, it begins to shape its own personality, eventually creating its own spirit.

Some say the shaman who uses the seguro will learn a song that only he or she can sing to summon greater healing power and connect more deeply with faerie.

How to make your own seguro

You will first need a nice jar. It should be made of glass, in a shape and style you like. You will also need a lid for it, such as a cork, but avoid metal lids and the jar opening must be big enough to look into or listen to when held up to your ear. You can reuse a food jar, just make sure it is clean. I have used an old large jar that had a candle in.

Once you have found a bottle you feel matches you in temperament and energy, clear the bottle of any negative energies it may carry.

Each day spend some time holding the seguro. Hum its song again if you think you hear it. As you do this, keep your mind focused on the goal of this magical entity you are creating: a seguro to help you in healing.

Meditate with the seguro. Your seguro is:

Your healing partner
A way for the fey to communicate with you

A source of healing and/or faery song
A friend who keeps your secrets
An ally who checks your fear
A source of knowledge when all other means fail

Start thinking about what you want to put in your seguro. Begin to collect natural objects that connect with you and that you feel would enhance your healing powers. What and how much you put in is up to you. It is best to be able to see light coming through the glass at some point, so don't fill it up completely. You really only need a small amount of each item, enough so that the total mixture covers the bottom of the bottle. You can always add new items later, or empty it and start over.

The basics of the seguro are ashes or salt, oil and plants or herbs. Ashes and salt are used for grounding and they will keep the healing images and words that come to you inside the bottle. Ashes and salt are also items with protective energy.

The herbs and/or plants you add will be communicated to you by faerie.

An essential oil or some rainwater or spring water might be suggested. Or faerie may recognise a place where your skills are weak and suggest a plant that will help you fill the gap. Follow the instructions given to you by the fae.

As you add each item to the seguro state its purpose out loud and charge it with your intent. When the seguro is complete, put the stopper in.

Your seguro is ready for use, whenever you need to consult it for wisdom, guidance or healing.

When you are not using your seguro, keep it covered with a cloth. But make sure you visit it regularly to connect with the energies and to strengthen your bond with it.

Faerie guardians

Maybe you like the idea of a faerie guardian – a fae guardian can form a focus for your own innate power and wisdom, amplified by the aspect of nature that is represented by the faerie. If you select a faerie form now, it may serve you for a few days, weeks, months or years. Because the fae can shapeshift, your guardian may appear as an animal or bird, or sometimes reside in a tree in your garden.

You may also like to work with the Faerie King and Queen too. Many Faerie Queens are linked to Goddesses. Many Goddesses are described not only as a Faerie Goddess but also as Queen of the Faeries.

What about the Faerie King? These have been described as demoted Celtic Gods who were forgotten and faded into the realms of faerie land.

A warning – I would suggest you always work with protection when working with the fae. Laziness and complacency when working with faeries can lead to undesirable results. Perform protection and grounding routines every time!

And of course, NEVER dance or partake of food and drink when on a visit to the realm of the fae! This can lead to entrapment. Although I have heard that witches are said to be among the only mortals who may blur these rules slightly, it has never been tested.

Faerie meditation

If you haven't worked with faerie before, it might be wise to cast a protective circle of light around yourself before you begin this meditation. If possible, it also helps to be outside somewhere in nature while you do this meditation, even if it is just sitting in your garden. I would also suggest that on a first meeting you don't follow the fae to its home if it invites you.

Make yourself comfortable, close your eyes and focus on your breathing, deep breaths in… deep breaths out…

As the world around you dissipates you find yourself sitting at the base of a small hill, the sun is shining and the air is warm with a lovely blue sky above you. It is summer and you are surrounded by lots of beautiful flowers and trees.

You sit quietly just watching the butterflies and the bees hopping from flower to flower.

Send out a quiet message to the fae; ask if there is anyone who would come to meet you…

Keep sitting quietly, keep watching the flowers, the trees and any birds, insects or animals you see – sometimes the fae can shapeshift…

You may have to sit a while, you may have to finish the meditation and come back to it another time.

However if a fae appears to you, be polite and sit and chat…

When you are ready say your farewells and slowly bring yourself back to reality.

Open your eyes, wriggle your fingers and toes, stretch your arms and legs. Don't forget to ground.

Chapter 30

The Elementals

The elementals are the energies of nature itself; they are the forces of the elements. They are true energy and have the characteristics of the element they belong to. They can take on any shape, size or form to deal with a particular task.

Elementals can charge us with energy; they can work with us on a physical, mental, emotional and spiritual level. Learning to work with them can tune us in to connect with the energy of nature around us. The elementals interweave their energy patterns to create and keep all of nature, all of life on our planet.

As with faeries, elementals have nothing to obstruct them, they can move through matter with ease, but they also need to connect with us to help with their own spiritual growth and evolution.

Earth elementals – gnomes

The gnome is the archetypal spirit of earth. Try not to think of the gnome you know from faerie stories, elemental gnomes are very earthy but their form and shape can vary immensely and they can change to suit their situation.

Earth elementals maintain our planet, the structure itself. They create the forests, the trees, the plants and the flowers. They design all the crystals and rocks, they are very skilled craftsmen. They work very closely with nature. They are the beings that put the energy into all the rocks, pebbles and crystals.

An earth elemental can help us attune to nature; they can work with us to help maintain our own physical bodies. They can help us develop all of our senses, to look after ourselves, to feel grounded and connected. Working with them can give us determination, appreciation, openness and spontaneity.

Be careful though, too much work with just the earth elementals and you might find yourself feeling cynical, sceptical and overly cautious.

Water elementals – undines

These elementals are the force of water. It can be springs, rivers, oceans, lakes, wherever there is a source of natural water. Water is life, we can't survive without it. The water elementals can help us find our inner source, they can help us find and work with our empathy, healing and purification.

An undine is a water sprite of sorts, more primal than a mermaid (or merman) but more developed than a basic water sprite – somewhere in between!

Undines work to keep our astral bodies in shape, to help us feel the connection to nature. They help us open up to our psychic abilities, our emotions, creativity, intuition and imagination. They help us to live life to the full and experience all that is available to us.

If you dream of water, the sea or rivers that could be the undines at work. Ask for their help in dream work, they can aid you in lucid dreaming and astral travel.

Not connecting with the undines regularly can cause us to become unbalanced and we could find our bodies clogging up with toxins.

But again, be careful, as too much work with the undines can cause us to become overly emotional. On a physical level it can also manifest as water retention. You may become self absorbed and your imagination might run away with you, making you overly sensitive and fearful.

Air elementals – sylphs

These beings are the embodiment of air, they are similar to faeries and angels and they often do work directly with angels.

They are creativity; they are the source of life energy, what we might call prana or chi. We cannot live without air.

Sylphs are very intelligent, they create the atmosphere itself.

Sylphs do a lot of healing work, they can help alleviate pain and ease suffering, but they also work to prompt inspiration and creativity. They work to help us fulfil our mental capacity to the fullest, they help us become inspired and seek knowledge. They clear out negative thoughts and keep our spirits up. They work with our intuition and our common sense.

Air elementals also care for our physical bodies by helping us to breathe.

As with all the elementals, too much exposure to sylphs can cause problems, it can make our minds overly active, we may procrastinate too much, we might become highly strung and extremely nervous, never settling on one thing and always wanting to change.

Fire elementals – salamanders

Salamanders are the embodiment of fire. Any flame has the spirit of a fire elemental within it. They control all fires, all flames, lightning, heat, volcanoes and any explosions.

Don't think of a salamander as being the lizard type creature, but think of a flame as it twists and turns like a serpent.

Fire elementals create very powerful emotions within us, they put the spark of spiritual ideas into our heads and hearts, they are the power that burns old habits and ideals and creates new ones. Fire destructs and makes way for the new.

Fire elementals work with us for healing; they can detox the body. But we must be careful as their energy is very strong and not easy to control (think about a fire getting out of hand and how difficult it is to control). They also use their energy to help our spiritual selves, they work with our spiritual energy, and they also stimulate our faith and enthusiasm and open us up to psychic insight and perception. Working with the salamander can help with vitality and loyalty, making you assertive, spiritual and full of aspiration.

Not being connected with your fire elemental can cause lack of self control, restlessness, and burn out, no patience, distrust and pessimism.

On a physical level salamanders aid our circulation and body temperature, assisting our metabolism.

Attuning to the elementals

You may find that you are automatically drawn to one elemental more than the others. The ultimate goal is to be balanced with all of them.

Usually you will find the elemental that you are drawn to is connected to your sign of the zodiac. That elemental will probably be the easiest one for you to work with.

All the elementals work well with each other; you just need to figure out how to work with them all together in balance.

If you find, after you have worked out which elemental groups you have with you, that one or two elemental groups are missing, you might want to spend a bit of time making sure you work with that group or groups too to make sure you get complete balance.

Another way to check which elemental groups you need to pay more attention to is to make a list as suggested in the Elements chapter.

Once you have worked out which elemental is your main one, you will want to start making a connection. You can do this with the help of a meditation.

Research your elemental, find out all about that group and its correspondences; find out any information associated with it.

If at all possible go to a place outside in nature that feels like that element, even if it is just sitting in your garden bare foot for earth, or sitting by the local pond for water. If that isn't possible get a picture up on your computer that shouts out that element to you.

Earth elemental meditation

Make yourself comfortable, close your eyes and focus on your breathing, deep breaths in... deep breaths out...

As your world around you dissipates, you find yourself in a crystal cave, every surface is covered in beautiful sparkling coloured crystals, and interspersed with candles so that the flames flicker and shine off the facets of the walls and ceiling.

Beneath your feet is earth, rich, dark brown soil and you can smell its earthy tones.

The air is cool but not cold.

You turn slowly around, taking in the wondrous sight, the walls, the ceiling, the glint of the candle flames on every crystal, it is breathtaking.

You walk to one of the walls and put your hand out to feel the crystals, you connect with the earth energy.

Then as you are looking around, a small man comes out of a tunnel you had not noticed before. You take in his appearance. What is he wearing? How old does he look? What impression do you get from him?

He greets you and welcomes you to the cave. He invites you to sit with him and talk...

When you are finished you thank him and bid farewell.

Take one last look around the cave, and then slowly and gently bring yourself back to your reality.

Wriggling your fingers and toes and stretching your arms and legs, open your eyes. Ground.

Air elemental meditation

Make yourself comfortable, close your eyes and focus on your breathing, deep breaths in... deep breaths out...

As your world around you dissipates you find yourself floating in a clear blue sky, surrounded by beautiful light white clouds. You are not scared or worried; you are perfectly comfortable just floating in the air.

Breathe in the air, take in the sight, feel the breeze around you, feel the energy around you.

Then you notice a being floating towards you. What do they look like? What impression do you get from them?

They greet you and gesture for you to rest awhile with them on a nearby cloud; you are surprised that it becomes solid as you sit on it. You sit with the air elemental and talk…

When you are ready, thank the being and bid farewell.

Take one last look around you, and then slowly and gently bring yourself back to your reality.

Wriggling your fingers and toes and stretching your arms and legs, open your eyes. Ground.

Fire elemental meditation

Make yourself comfortable, close your eyes and focus on your breathing, deep breaths in… deep breaths out…

As your world around you dissipates you find yourself in a desert. The sun is hot and you can feel the warm, dry heat around you and the hot sand beneath your feet.

Look around you, the sand stretches out for miles, interspersed occasionally with a lone tree.

Feel the heat, feel the sun on your skin, and feel the energy from beneath your feet, the energy of fire.

You can hear someone or something coming so you turn to see what can only be a fire elemental. What do they look like? What impressions and feelings do you get from them?

The being invites you to sit a while and chat, gesturing to a large flat rock for you to seat yourself on…

When you are ready thank the being and bid farewell.

Take one last look around you, and then slowly and gently bring yourself back to your reality.

Wriggling your fingers and toes and stretching your arms and legs, open your eyes. Ground.

Water elemental meditation

Make yourself comfortable, close your eyes and focus on your breathing, deep breaths in… deep breaths out…

As your world around you dissipates you find yourself beside a deep blue lagoon in the middle of a dense jungle, the air is hot and moist.

The lagoon is an amazing azure blue colour and the sunlight sparkles on the surface.

You sit on the rocks beside the lagoon and dip your hand into the beautiful blue water, it is cool and refreshing, feel the energy from it… connect with it…

You hear a splash and look up to see a being emerging from the water. They make their way towards you with a greeting and an invitation to sit a while and chat…

What do they look like? What impressions do you get from them?

When you are ready take a last look around your setting, thank the being and bid them farewell.

Slowly and gently bring yourself back to your reality.

Wriggling your fingers and toes and stretching your arms and legs, open your eyes. Ground.

Chapter 31

Nature Spirits

The world of faerie covers a huge number of beings and those include nature spirits.

We can be multidimensional beings; unfortunately most people choose not to be. Venturing between worlds can be challenging, but it can be so very rewarding too. I personally believe that nature spirits are one of the easiest of the fae to connect with.

What is the difference between elementals and nature spirits?

Elementals are the corner stones of nature, they have each element strongly flowing through them, they are pure energy but they don't really have personalities. We can connect with them and we will feel the element that they work with, but it is on a basic level.

Nature spirits are also sometimes referred to as elves and as a generalisation, faeries. Nature spirits are also connected with the elements and they are usually found close to one of the elements in nature itself. Wood elves can be found in forests and water spirits can be found by streams and ponds.

A faerie shaman will work directly with nature spirits for healing. The spirit of each plant or flower is called upon for assistance with healing work. This is either done in the form of herbalism, using the plants leaves, flowers or roots in spells, lotions or potions or it can be as a request that the nature spirit sends its healing energy to the patient.

So let's look at nature spirits in more detail...

Earth nature spirits

These include wood and tree elves, flower faeries, brownies and dwarves. All of these spirits will be connected with or work with the element of earth in some way.

Think of a dwarf and you will see the connection to the earth element. They often live and/or work in caves or underground, they are usually craftsmen of some sort whether it is working with metals or stone. They usually like to hoard treasures.

Trolls are also considered to be earth nature spirits, but don't be swayed by the Disney idea of a large ugly creature living under a bridge, Scandinavian trolls are elves.

Our environment is looked after by field and flower faeries and elves. They create, tend and live in the fields, trees, grasses, shrubs and flowers on this planet. Generally they are light and kind hearted but woe betide anyone who damages their habitat for no good reason or without asking permission from them first!

Stones, pebbles and rocks also have earth nature spirits. Every pebble, every crystal, will have its very own elf or faerie spirit. Some of the really old rocks will have stone devas; they will be very wise.

Trees of course have tree spirits, each tree having its own one, but trees will also provide homes for all sorts of nature spirits with different trees attracting different types of the fae.

Earth nature spirits can teach us many things, practical abilities, to be grounded, how to plant and grow not just herbs or flowers but things within our lives too. They can show us how to connect with Mother Earth and how to be less materialistic.

Earth nature spirits will inspire us to go for goal, to have determination, to seek balance and to connect with nature and how to work with her energies.

How to connect with earth nature spirits

Preferably take yourself outside for this exercise. It doesn't matter if it is in a field, a forest or in your own back garden, but you need to be somewhere that you can connect your hands and/or feet with the earth. If it is not practical for you to be outside, bring some soil indoors or use the soil that you have in a pot plant.

Make sure you won't be disturbed and make yourself comfortable. You can sit or stand, it is up to you.

Place your hands or your feet on the earth. Take some time to really feel the connection between yourself and the earth, feel the energy.

Make yourself comfortable, relax and focus on your breathing, deep breaths in... deep breaths out...

Depending on your location you can either close your eyes or not. If you are in a very earthy setting then keep them open, if not close them so that you can visualise.

Then either look at your surrounds – trees, soil, fields etc or visualise yourself in that kind of environment.

Feel the energy around you, connect with the earth element from the trees, the grass, the plants and flowers, really feel it.

Then ask if there are any nature spirits that wish to meet you.

If you have your eyes open you might see a glimmer or a flicker out of the corner of your eye at this point. You may just hear a voice. You may just get the feeling that someone is there with you.

Wait and see if anyone wants to connect with you.

If you are lucky enough to make contact, ask whatever questions you would like to, or just converse, but please make sure you are polite and courteous. You don't want to upset the fae, they can be pesky creatures when annoyed (as we all can!)

Once you have finished your conversation bid your farewell to the nature spirit and slowly bring yourself back to our world.

If you don't connect this time, don't worry you can try again another time.

Water nature spirits

Water sprites, faeries or spirits can be found in the oceans, rivers, lakes, ponds, streams and waterfalls. They are generally quite beautiful beings.

Water nature spirits can help you with purification, changes, life and death, mysteries, healing and magic. They can also help with emotional problems and situations, music, inspiration, intuition and imagination. We can learn how to nurture, to become flexible in our ways, to awaken our romantic side and to work with our compassion.

Connecting with a water nature spirit can be very energising; they love to heal and are usually more than happy to send energy our way.

Water nature spirits look after all aquatic creatures and the sources of the water that they live in or by.

Pools of water can also be gateways into other realms.

Freshwater nature spirits are usually more genteel than those of salt water, but all the spirits will vary and take on the characteristics of the water and environment that they are surrounded by.

Water nature spirits – nymphs, selkies, kelpies and the like – are all known for being able to shapeshift, sometimes into human form, other times into animals.

These spirits also like company. Although you will sometimes find solitary water spirits, you will more often find them in groups.

How to connect with water nature spirits

For this you really need to be by a source of water if you can, a pond or lake, the ocean even a puddle or a bowl of rainwater you have collected. If it is winter and you have snow or ice you could collect some of that to use.

Again make sure you won't be disturbed and make yourself comfortable.

Place your hands or your feet into the water or splash some of the water onto your face. Take some time to really feel and connect with the energy that the water holds within.

Then if you are in a suitable location look at the water, watch the waves or the ripples.

Focus on your breathing, deep breaths in… deep breaths out…

Visualise yourself walking into a large lake or the ocean; connect even more with the element of water as you start to swim.

As you swim keep an eye out for aquatic creatures that might come to greet you, then ask if there are any water spirits that would like to meet with you. Watch and see who comes.

If you are lucky enough to connect with a water spirit take some time to converse, but be mindful of being polite, treat them with respect.

Once you have finished your conversation, make your farewell and swim back to the shore.

Then slowly bring yourself back to this world.

Again, if you didn't connect with a water nature spirit this time, try again on another occasion.

Air nature spirits

Air nature spirits can be tiny wisps of breeze right up to powerful storm faeries. These spirits are free and can be found almost anywhere.

Air nature spirits love to heal, they like working as guardians and love children (not to eat, but to work with!) These spirits help us, as humans, to learn and grow. Air spirits can help us work with our minds, to empower ourselves and channel our thoughts. They can aid us in our spiritual journeys. They inspire wisdom, musical abilities, inner strength and languages. The air nature spirits also bring wishes.

Air nature spirits look after the atmosphere, the air we breathe and the weather.

Air spirits are delicate and beautiful, often being mistaken for angels. They like to use clairaudience to connect with us. They love poetry, songs and stories.

Air spirits can also shapeshift, their preferred choice being that of butterflies, birds or insects.

You can tell if an air spirit is near by a sudden breeze, a wisp of air on a still day or the finding of a lone feather on the ground.

How to connect with an air spirit

You don't need any particular items for this exercise, but you do really need to be outside, preferably when there is a breeze of some sort.

Make sure you won't be disturbed and make yourself comfortable.

Focus on your breathing and connect with the air that you are taking into your lungs. Feel the breeze on your face, your arms, and your legs; really connect with the energy of the element of air. Feel the power that air has within.

Close your eyes and visualise yourself standing on top of a hill or mountain, feel the wind swirling around you.

See the clouds in the sky above you.

Ask if there are any air nature spirits that would like to come to meet you. Wait, and if you are lucky enough converse with them, remember as always to be respectful.

Once you are finished with your conversation, bid your farewell.

Slowly come back to this world.

If you didn't connect with a spirit this time, try again at a later date.

Fire nature spirits

Fire nature spirits can be found in all sorts of places within our everyday lives. There are the obvious places such as flames in your bonfire, fireplaces and candle flames. On a larger scale there are volcanoes and lava as well. But fire nature spirits can also be found in the smoke and rays of sunlight. And, of course, we all have an inner 'spark' or 'flame'.

Fire nature spirits not only take care of flames, lava and such things as lightning, they also help us with our passion, courage, sexuality, creativity, physical energy, heat within our bodies and our spiritual passion. They inspire, support and encourage change and transformation. They can teach us about life, death and renewal. Fire spirits also show us our true inner self – warts and all. We might not always like what they show us, but we should always take note and learn from what we see.

Fire nature spirits are considered to be the most difficult of the nature spirits to work with. Fire is creative but destructive too and their characters reflect this. They are also highly intelligent and incredibly independent. And, of course, fire does not stand still… ever, neither do fire spirits!

If a fire spirit shapeshifts at all, mostly they don't tend to, but if they do it will be in the form of a dragon, a phoenix, a snake or a reptile.

How to connect with a fire nature spirit

This exercise can be performed outside if you have space for a bonfire, or have a fire pit or chimenea that you can light. Otherwise sit inside and light at least one candle, preferably more than one.

Make sure you won't be disturbed and make yourself comfortable. Focus on your breathing, deep breaths in… deep breaths out…

Focus on your candle flames or the flames from the fire. Really connect with every aspect of the energy of the element of fire, feel it, smell it, make that connection. Watch the flame as it dances and moves.

Ask if there is a fire nature spirit that would meet with you. Hopefully one will make itself known and you can converse, but as always be polite and respectful.

Once you have had your conversation bid your farewell.

Slowly come back to this world.

If you did not connect with a fire spirit this time, try again at another time.

Flower faeries

Flower faeries and elves are some of the most beautiful spirits. They can be all sorts of colours and often resemble the flowers that they connect with.

These flower spirits create the flowers from the ground up. They help them grow, and they design the colours, the shapes and the fragrances.

Each and every single flower will have its own flower spirit. The flower spirit will be responsible for the growth, health and maintenance of that particular plant.

Flower spirits can help us with healing, inspiration and energy.

Don't worry about picking a flower from your garden, the flower spirit will continue to look after it. But do remove dead or dying flowers from you house as the flower spirits will look for energy from you to help with the natural breakdown of the flower and that will leave you feeling tired and drawn.

If you are picking wild flowers from fields, woodlands and hedgerows, do remember that some of them are protected and never take very many, make sure to leave enough for others to enjoy. Remember the flower faerie will travel home with the flower.

In the case of plants in your garden that are perennial, the flower spirit will stay with that plant, even over the winter months, tending to it and helping it regain its strength for the spring.

If you are out and about and smell the fragrance of a flower on the air, or suddenly catch glimpse of a beautiful flower, this is the flower faeries trying to catch your attention.

Each flower spirit will have some of the characteristics of the flower it tends; it will also have its own unique personality so therefore each individual flower spirit will have its own particular energies to share with us.

To connect with flower faeries is simple. Work with plants in your garden, or with house plants. Learn how they grow. Keep fresh flowers in your home.

Connecting with particular flower faeries can help you take on their specific energies and qualities.

For instance flower spirits from a geranium can make you happy and will help guide you to strengthen your aura. Marigold flower spirits can help you with your psychic abilities and the rose flower spirit can help you with matters of love, divination and truth.

And it goes without saying that if you care for the plants and flowers in your home and garden then the nature spirits will flourish.

If you forget to water, or don't look after them, you may find that the nature spirits start to cause mischief for you.

How to connect with a flower nature spirit

For this you will need a flowering plant or some fresh cut flowers.

Relax and make yourself comfortable. Focus on your breathing, deep breaths in… deep breaths out…

Select a flower to focus on. Look at the colour, the shape, feel the texture and take in the fragrance.

Really connect with the essence of the flower.

Ask if the flower nature spirit will come and meet you.

Hopefully it will and you may converse, but be polite and respectful.

Once you have had your conversation, bid your farewell.

Slowly come back to this world.

If you did not connect this time, try with another flower.

Tree spirits

All trees have a nature spirit within them just as the flowers do. The tree spirit is called a dryad and is born with the tree, grows with it and dies when the tree does; it has all the characteristics and personality of the particular tree it is connected to.

Desert nature spirits

Do not forget those nature spirits that live in the dry deserts. These fae are beautifully exotic, usually naked and mostly faintly transparent to the eye.

The desert spirits look after all and any plants that grow in their environment, even the smallest plant will get their nurturing attention.

Ice and snow nature spirits

On the flip side of the desert spirits, we have the ice and snow spirits. They create the snow, the ice and icicles. They make the pretty icy patterns in the winter.

Wherever there is nature there is a spirit from the realm of faerie to tend to it.

Chapter 32

Colour Magic

In most of the items that I make for spell work I find that I automatically correspond the colour of the materials used to the intent. Corresponding the colour to your intent can add a huge amount of power to your spell working, whether it is in the form of the colour of candle, the colour of crystals used or the colour of medicine bag, it all adds that bit extra.

Here is a guide that I use:

Black: protection, ward negativity, remove hexes, spirit contact, truth, remove discord or confusion and binding for spell work

Dark blue: the Goddess, water elemental, truth, dreams, protection, change, meditation, healing

Light blue: psychic awareness, intuition, opportunity, understanding, safe journey, patience, tranquillity, ward depression, healing, health

Brown: endurance, houses and homes, uncertainties, influence friendships

Green: earth elemental, nature magic, luck, fertility, healing, balance, courage, work, prosperity, changing directions or attitudes

Indigo: meditation, spirit communication, karma workings, neutralise baneful magic, ward slander

Lilac: spiritual development, psychic growth, divination, Otherworld

Orange: the God, strength, healing, attracting things, vitality, adaptability, luck, encouragement, clearing the mind, justice, career goals, legal matters, selling, action, ambition, general success

Pink: honour, morality, friendships, emotional love, social ability, good will, caring, healing emotions, peace, affection, nurturing, romance and partnerships

Purple: power, spirit, spiritual development, intuition, ambition, healing, wisdom, progress, business, spirit communication, protection, occultism, self assurance

Red: fire elemental, strength, power, energy, health, vigour, enthusiasm, courage, passion, sexuality, vibrancy, survival, driving force

White: purity, protection, truth, meditation, peace, sincerity, justice, ward doubt and fear

Yellow: air elemental, divination, clairvoyance, mental alertness, intellect, memory, prosperity, learning, changes, harmony, creativity, self promotion

Sometimes I look up the list, some I remember; mostly I go by instinct and then when I check I realise my instinct is bang on the mark. This is just my idea of a list of correspondences, others may use different colours – it is a personal thing, go with what feels right for you.

Chapter 33

Hexes and Banishing

I suspect a huge chunk of society when they think of a witch, see us as old crones pointing a bony finger and sending out a wicked curse. I am sure there are a few witches who actually do that, and people that we would like to do it to on occasion… but I am not going to advocate that particularly, what I want to do is share knowledge. Knowledge is power and if you know about curses and hexes then you are forewarned and forearmed. If you choose to hex or curse then that of course is your right to do so, just be mindful of the backlash…

I am also not going to get on a soapbox and spout off about morals, taking the high ground and mentioning karma etc – that choice is yours to make, and yours alone.

My personal thoughts are if you get cross or upset about something or with someone… stop… think… don't just blindly work a spell to curse or hex someone in the heat of anger. Let the hurt die down first, and then decide what course of action to take.

Sometimes there are situations that warrant a particular action or reaction and sometimes it is not easy to decide what course to follow. A good rule of thumb to follow is if you would not do it in reality then don't do it with magic. Make sure that what you do, whatever kind of defensive action you take, is equivalent to the action that was taken against you. You would not blow up someone's car just for stepping on your toe would you? Think about your plan, if you feel uncomfortable in any way then don't do it, go back to the drawing board and come up with Plan B, C or D (and all the rest of the letters in the alphabet if need be!)

Curses and hexes are not for the faint hearted and if you

decide that is the path you want to go down, I urge you to not take them lightly and never chuck them about willy nilly – take responsibility for your actions. You also need to be very, very sure that the person you are sending a curse or hex to is the person responsible…

OK so let's take a look at what hexes and curses are:

Just as there are hundreds and thousands of love and prosperity spells, there are probably just as many curses. Some of them involve long complicated rituals, some require all sorts of ingredients and some are just gestures with a hand or a word.

So what is the difference between a hex and a curse? Well, I am not sure there is much of a difference to be honest, just different names from different cultures. However, the general consensus seems to be that a hex is a spell or bewitchment and comes from Pennsylvania Dutch folklore. Traditionally they could be good or bad and a witch could be paid to provide one. A curse is a malevolent spell that is cast with the purpose of inflicting harm upon another; curses can be spoken or written. Objects can also be cursed to cause bad luck, misfortune, ill health and even death.

Essentially it is the wilful direction of negative energy towards someone with the intent to harm. Usually hexes and curses take some time to develop, building up slowly. However, if you are well shielded and protected you are very unlikely to become the victim of a hex yourself and I think it happens a lot less frequently than people believe!

I have included some curses and hexes. Again I advise you to think carefully before using them, and they are here so that you have knowledge of what they are and how they are created.

Cursing stones

Charging a stone with malevolence is an ancient Celtic method of delivering a curse.

This is done when you are feeling full of negative emotions

such as rage, anger and hatred; you direct all those emotions into the stone. It can then be stored and used later by taking up the stone in your hands, turning it widdershins and directing those emotions to where you want them to go.

(This is also a useful way of venting all that anger and frustration. By sending it into the stone, you could then drop it into the sea or a river so that those negative emotions wash away.)

A misfortune hex

Write the name of your enemy on a piece of paper in black ink. Write the name nine times. Light a black candle and say out loud:

I curse and hex thee (name of enemy)
Let it be done

Then light the piece of paper in the candle flame and drop it into a fireproof container to burn out.

To break a hex

If you feel that you have been hexed, this should break the link and return it to the caster.

You will need:

A sprig of rosemary
A piece of paper
A red pen
Scissors
A piece of red cloth
Paprika or chilli pepper
Red cotton

Keep the rosemary on your person while you work this hex. Write the name of the person who has hexed you on a piece of paper. If you don't know who did it just write 'enemy mine'. With the red pen, draw a doll shape around the name and cut it out. Lay the paper doll face down on the red cloth and sprinkle it with paprika. Tie the cotton around the middle of the doll then wrap it in the red cloth, hold it in your hands and say:

Enemy mine your power is gone
The hex is broken, the spell undone
Enemy mine go away
So shall it be from this day
This spell will last until your apology sets you free by me
This is my will, so mote it be

Perform this chant for seven nights in a row, then unwrap the doll, tear it into nine pieces and burn it. Scatter the ashes somewhere away from your home and dispose of the red cloth.

Binding

I would like to also look at binding. This is a form of spell that binds a person or situation so that they or it can no longer harm you. I have found this form of working particularly successful. As long as you are pure in your intent, it doesn't actually harm the person or cause them any discomfort, it just stops them from hurting or harassing you. But bear in mind that this spell does take away the free will of the person you are binding, so use with caution.

A binding spell can be very simple – you use an object that represents the person causing you harm – it can be a poppet, it could be a photograph or it could just be a lump of clay that you have identified as the person. It can then be bound with string, ribbon or even sticky tape. As you bind the object visualise binding the harmful energies of that person and speak your wishes, that the person can no longer harm you or harass you. Bury the spell.

A cord binding spell

Cast a circle, using cord or string, then think of what you what you want to bind. Say in a strong voice:

The first knot binds my intention.
The second knot binds ill-wishing
The third knot binds it all.
These knots shall hold the spell,
Until these knots are all undone.

As you speak a line, tie one knot. The first knot should be at one end, while the second in the middle. The final knot should be placed at the other end. As you tie the knots, visualise what you are binding being stopped from doing harm. Once the knots are tied, see the spell being continued until the knots are untied.

To unbind a binding spell

Some binding spells can cause physical effects. You might feel that you have invisible strands of hair or thin strings wrapped around you. You won't be able see them but you will feel them and nothing you do can make that sensation stop. Here is a way to dispel a binding:

Cut a small piece of your own hair and put it in a bowl.
Light three candles – one red, one white and one green.
In a fire safe bowl or cauldron, light a piece of charcoal and add some myrrh, patchouli and sandalwood incense
Take a sterile needle or pin and prick your right index finger.
Squeeze three drops of blood into the incense.
As you drop the hair onto the incense repeat these words:

With blood, candle and scent times three
No longer shall this binding be
Free to live and free to soar

Let me leave the house once more.
As I burn this hair, a part of me
Let my heart and soul be free!
As is my will, so mote it be!

Let the incense burn out and scatter the ashes outside.

Banishing

And on to banishing. Now, as I mentioned earlier, I have had a lot of experience with this and not all of it has been good. I thought it sounded like a lovely idea to 'banish negative energy' from my life. What I didn't expect was the huge circle that this banishing covers. It does not just get rid of bad luck it covers all sorts of things… including people. To banish all negative energy from your life is not always a good thing. We all need a balance in life, for instance think about batteries. They need positive and negative to work, and if you took away the negative they would have no power.

Much better to ask that 'any negative energy that serves me no good' be released, it is safer believe me! Note I also used the word 'release' rather than 'banish', I have found that it is safer! But please be prepared for unexpected results…

A very simple banishing spell is to use some slips of paper and a cauldron. Write what you want to banish on the slips of paper, light the corner of each slip on a candle and drop it into the cauldron, visualising the feeling/emotion/bad habit/whatever disappearing. Send the ashes out into the wind or into running water (or even down the toilet).

Another simple idea is to write what you want to be rid of on a slip of paper and drop it into running water or again even to flush it down the toilet.

PLEASE remember that whatever you banish leaves a hole. That hole must be purposely filled with light and love otherwise it will just be replaced with that which is similar to what you wanted to get rid of in the first place. I find it wise to add onto the end of a banishing something like 'and fill the void with love, light and blessings'.

Remember that banishings sometimes take some time to work too.

Exorcism

Leading on from banishing is exorcism, meaning to drive out or ward off evil spirits – according to the dictionary anyway. I do think that the likelihood of evil or malevolent spirits haunting a place is very slim. I think that spirits get trapped or caught in places where they don't want to be and they get frightened or confused and don't know where to go.

I have experienced helping spirits to move on. One particular incident was in a small shop in Dorset. Things kept getting moved in the shop window and the owner, although not frightened, was concerned. I and a couple of friends (a witch and a druid) performed a small séance in the shop using a spirit board. Which caused a lot of confusion at first because the spirit turned out to be a young girl who couldn't read or write... However, it turned out she was killed in a fire in the house a couple of centuries before and didn't know what had happened or where her family had gone. She felt abandoned and confused. She was moving things about because she was crying out for help. We aided her and guided her to move on to the Summerlands. There was also another spirit in the shop, an elderly gentleman, who we made contact with. He didn't want to move on as he liked being there, but we made him promise not to cause any mischief!

A word of caution with exorcism. Bear in mind that just asking a spirit to move from the place they are in will only move them onto another place on this Earth. They need to be helped and guided to move on to the Otherworld.

In my experience you don't need lots of candles, crosses,

sacred water or Bibles. Just contacting the spirit and talking to them, then helping and guiding them in crossing over, is really all that is usually needed.

Hex signs

American folk magic has hex signs, but they aren't bad or evil. They are a form of protection, good luck or prosperity. They are usually geometric in shape and usually very pretty. A lot of them bear a resemblance to mandalas. They were hung outside or just inside the property to bring peace, love and prosperity to the home and to keep out bad luck.

Some symbols used in hex signs and their meanings:

Tulip: faith
Five-point star: protection, good luck
Eight-point star: Wheel of the Year
Hearts: love
Six-point star: protection referred to in German as hexefus which translated means 'witches foot'

Colours are important too and have pretty much the same correspondences as we use in colour magic.

Funnily enough some of the old hex signs were used to ward against witches…

Chapter 34

Dreaming and Astral Travel

Working with your dreams and understanding their meanings can be fascinating, as can lucid dreaming and astral travel, although the latter two can be quite difficult to master.

Let's start with dreaming...

Dreams are messages sent to your conscious mind from your subconscious and I think the best person to interpret the meanings of your dreams is YOU. There are lots of books out there that will give you the basic meanings of symbols seen in your dreams, but ultimately it is your dream and your mind and therefore you are best qualified to interpret the meaning.

A dream is made up of your thoughts, your concerns, your worries, your hopes, your wishes, your desires, your memories and maybe even events that have yet to happen.

Why are dreams often so muddled and confusing? Well the mind is a complicated thing, it has a lot of information stored and when we dream it tries to send all the information at once. It is then up to us to filter through it.

Everyone dreams. You might not always remember them, but we all do. Dreams can be a source of insight into ourselves; they can also help us cope with situations where we need a bit of guidance. Or they can just simply make us feel good (or bad depending on the type of dream).

How can you remember your dreams?

Yep, I know the feeling. You have had an amazing dream, but once you get out of bed it has vanished and no matter how hard you try to grab hold of those thoughts and images they are gone. OK, so there are a few hints and tips.

Just before you go to sleep charge a glass of water with your intent to recall your dream fully and completely on waking, drink the water and then lay down to sleep.

Place a crystal under your pillow that has the specific energies and qualities to help you recall your dreams.

As soon as you wake, don't move, lie still. Take a deep breath and recall the entire dream, replay it back in your mind, really 'feel' all the details, the images, the senses and the scents. Replaying it once you have woken, but not actually got up, helps to set the images into your conscious mind.

Keep a notebook beside your bed and when you wake, make sure you don't even sit up in bed, just grab the pad and jot down some notes, it doesn't have to be the whole novel just some key points to jog your memory once you are fully awake. You don't necessarily have to recall the entire dream; the key snap shots that seem important will be enough.

It is often quite interesting to keep a specific dream journal. Note down your dreams from each night; you can then refer back to them at a later date and hopefully glean a lot more information and insight from them.

When you recall your dream ask some questions:

What topic was my dream on?
What energy did it involve?
What was the most important part of the dream?
What message was it trying to convey to me?
How can I work with the information brought to me?
What parts of the dream are based in reality?
What parts of the dream really influence me?
Who was in the dream and who did they represent?
What did my senses feel? Heat/light/dark/cold etc
What voices did I hear?
What colours were in my dream?
Do I have any reoccurring themes or symbols in my dreams?

Lucid dreaming

What is lucid dreaming? Well, when we become aware of what we are dreaming and when we are able to interact with our dreams – that is lucid dreaming.

Once you are able to find your dream energy centre and how to work with it the more successful you will become at lucid dreaming.

Lucid dreaming is all about being in control of your dream, not in a 'control freak' kind of way, but in a way that you try to understand your dream and use the energy to help.

I think lucid dreaming is a step on from daydreaming or meditation visualisations. You can go into a lucid dream with a question or a query, approach it with an open mind and with the idea that the dream will be productive.

An important aspect of lucid dreaming is to have the ability to become aware when you are in the dream, that awareness then becomes your point of lucidity. You will need to study your own sleep patterns to work out the best time for you, when you can work with dream lucidity easily.

You will need to think about 'reality checks'. This will show you whether you are actually lucid dreaming or not. It might be something simple like touching the earth with your fingers. You know what that feels like in the real world so it is a good check in the dream world – if it feels right then you are lucid dreaming. Do something that you can recognise the feel of. Practice these reality checks in your mind first before you enter the dream state.

Actually staying in lucid dream mode does take some work. It is all about keeping that fine balance between being in the dream state, but being lucid enough to explore further. Stay calm and relaxed, follow where you believe it is taking you, and if you hit resistance take your dream in another direction.

Spinning is a useful technique for lucid dreaming. You start by spinning your whole body around a few times – not literally, but in your dream! Allow the energy that you build up to stop you from hitting awareness and waking up. As you spin feel the energy inside you, take that focus from being inward and move your focus outwards into your dream. With practice this will help you to maintain lucidity in your dreams.

Astral travel

Astral travel is sometimes called astral journeying, astral projection or an out-of-body experience. It means that the part of you, your true inner self, leaves your physical body and travels to another reality or another place.

Every living thing has an etheric counterpart. The lower etheric plane is quite a dangerous place, if you find yourself there during and out-of-body experience it is recommended to quickly raise your vibrations and change your trip by looking upwards to find a better level. It may be signified by a bright white light or lots of bright colours.

The higher etheric plane, sometimes called the high astral or spiritual plane, is a very spiritual place; this is where you will find incredibly wonderful spiritual beings.

I believe that there are many, many etheric planes in between the higher and the lower planes.

The astral plane itself is a very emotional place; we are after all sending our astral self there, which is full of emotions. Hopefully your astral experiences will be wonderful and interesting, but please beware that sometimes they can be a bit scary and occasionally unpleasant. It is our own level of vibrations that determine which level of plane we visit. Remember YOU are always in control.

So why would you want to astral travel? Well it is a good way of visiting those who have passed on, it is also a way of travelling to interesting places, to learn, to experience, to gain knowledge and insight. And of course the astral plane isn't restricted by time or dimension!

As I mentioned before, astral travel can be difficult. It can take some time to master. It does take practice. We can leave our physical body once we are in a very relaxed state, that moment just between sleeping and waking.

There are various methods for performing astral travel, below are some ideas.

Determine a location that you want to visit astrally. Sit in a comfortable position, somewhere quiet where you will not be disturbed. Focus on your breathing.

Method 1

When you are in a calm, centred and relaxed state, try to separate your astral body from your physical body, starting by visualising it floating a foot or so above your physical body. Then you can send your astral body to wherever you want to, visualise your destination and send your body there.

Method 2

Another method is to expand your body roughly half an inch with each breath. This is done only with visualisation, is fairly easy to do, and often produces fast results.

When you have expanded to roughly twice your normal size, continue the process with even greater dimensions. Inches become feet, and feet become miles, and so on. Don't worry too much about the actual act of leaving your body.

One variation of this technique consists of proceeding little by little. For example, the first few times you would only move your astral arms out of your physical body, a bit later your whole upper body and head, and so on. Always keep in mind that obtaining the remote information is your actual goal, regardless of how you get there, and not necessarily the act of buzzing around in an astral body.

Method 3

Start with the basics, using either of the methods above to separate your astral body, but instead of disappearing off to the seaside; take an astral walk around your home. Feel your astral body strolling around the rooms in your house and remotely viewing all that they contain.

Returning

Once you want to return your astral body to your physical one, ask for permission first, and then slowly reconnect. Take your time doing this as you don't want to leave anything disconnected!

Chapter 35

Planetary Magic

Planetary magic is another one of those subjects within the Craft that is huge and people spend entire lifetimes working with it, but here is an introduction to working magic with the power of the planets.

Using the energy of planets within your magic, your rituals, spell casting and even incense and oil making will add power.

The seven basic planetary correspondences are Saturn, Jupiter, Mars, the Sun, Venus, Mercury and the Moon. Each planet is associated with qualities that we may wish to attract, symbols, materials and objects that are associated with each planet and help to channel that particular planetary influence. Each planet also corresponds with a day of the week (among other things) so it is useful to bear these in mind when working spells as well.

The symbols of these planets can be carved into candles or wands, or drawn on paper or in the air for spells, their uses are limitless.

In the Western Occult Tradition, each planet has traditionally possessed both a spirit and an intelligence: ethereal souls (sometimes called daemons) responsible for the baleful and beneficial influences (respectively) of the individual planet.

After all, even humans have souls, and the planets of the celestial realm are far more spiritual, existing closer to the Gods and constructed of a much more rarefied matter. It was therefore logical to occultists that the planets also possessed their own souls.

Mars

Positive: success in battles, judgements and petitions, victory against enemies, stopping of blood, sports, winning, resolve quarrels, gain courage, take action

Negative: hinders buildings, honours and riches, causes discord, strife and hatred, misfortune for hunters and fighters, barrenness and infertility

Zodiac sign: Aries and Scorpio

Day: Tuesday

Element: fire

Saturn

Positive: safety, power and success of petitions, intellect, good fortune, success in financial matters, buildings, towns and groups, banish negativity, overcome quarrels, banish illness, situations involving those in authority, paternal situations

Negative: hinders building and plantings i.e. growth, causes discord and quarrels, disperses armies. Saturn was traditionally held as an unfortunate planet and strongly associated with melancholy.

Zodiac signs: Capricorn and Aquarius

Day: Saturday

Elements: earth, water

Jupiter

Positive: gains and riches, favour and love, peace, concord, appeasement of enemies, confirmation of honours, dignities and counsels, dissolving of enchantments, expanding projects, find and work with spirituality, good health, long-term prosperity, make new friends, compassion

Negative: lack of energy, physical problems and loss of money

Zodiac signs: Sagittarius and Pisces

Day: Thursday

Elements: air, fire

Sun

Positive: being renowned, amiable, acceptable, potent in all works, equals a man to kings, good fortunes, success in all endeavours, wealth, will, gain, prosperity, dissolve painful or hostile relationships, make friends, find love, power

Negative: causes a man to be a tyrant, proud, ambitious, unsatisfiable, and to have an ill ending

Zodiac sign: Leo

Day: Sunday

Element: fire

Venus

Positive: encourages concord, ends strife, procures love, aids in conception, works against barrenness, dissolves enchantments, brings peace, makes all kind of animals fruitful, cures melancholy, brings joy, and good fortune, fast cash, work with your hands or mind with the arts, education

Negative: encourages strife, drives away a woman's love, blocks conception, encourages barrenness, brings bad luck, destroys joy, encourages melancholy

Zodiac signs: Taurus and Libra

Day: Friday

Elements: earth, water

Mercury

Positive: gratefulness, fortunate, brings gain, prevents poverty, helps memory, understanding and divination, encourages occult understanding through dreams, communication of all kinds, eloquence in speech or writing, study, science, divination, work with computers

Negative: brings ungratefulness and unfortunate activities, encourages poverty, drives away gains and inhibits memory, understanding and divination

Zodiac signs: Gemini and Virgo

Day: Wednesday
Element: air

Moon

Positive: gratefulness, amiable, pleasant, cheerful, honoured, removes malice and ill will, security during travel, increase of riches, bodily health, drives away enemies and other evil things, any water issues, finding lost objects, emotions, divination, maternal situations
Negative: renders a location unfortunate, causes people to flee from it, hinders physicians and people in offices
Zodiac sign: Cancer
Day: Monday
Element: water

Seven-day spells

A classic magic spell, usually involving a candle, is a seven-day spell. The magic is worked on a particular day and then repeated each day thereafter for seven days. This type of spell uses the energies of the seven days and the seven planets. Each day the magic and the energies of that day/planet building up until on the last day you have the power of all the seven classic planets.

You can use one taper candle with seven notches marked into it or seven smaller candles, whatever works for you.

Firstly you will need to decide what day of the week to start your spell on and work out all the energies and planets that tie in with each day. You will also need to write yourself a short invocation for each day, drawing upon the particular energies for each day and planet that it corresponds with.

Each day start with calming, grounding and centring yourself.

Cast a circle and call the quarters if you wish to.

Light your candle and quote your invocation. Say it three times; the first time to declare your intent and summon assistance from spirit, the second time banishes any unwanted energies and the third time it will send out the intent and seal the spell.

Do this for seven days, using your corresponding invocation on each day.

What about these retrogrades?

Well astrology is not my chosen subject, but a while back I decided I needed to find out what all this retrograde hype was about. Basically retrograde means when the planet goes backwards. A planet will appear to move backwards in the skies for a period of time – this is called a retrograde. I know they seem to get a bit of bad press, but they can give you a lot of long-term energy if you work with it rather than against it.

The appearance of retrograde motion is an illusion created by the orbit of planet Earth. The planets never really go backwards, it just looks like they do.

All of the planets within our solar system seem to stop at various times and then to move backwards. After a while they stop again and appear to move forward again. Because some planets have faster orbits than others, the time they stop, turn retrograde and stop and then turn again varies from planet to planet.

So how does that affect us? Well retrograde is the universe saying to us – time to hold fire for a bit, sit back, put your feet up and take a load off. Obviously with our busy lives we can't do this so we have to work with it.

How do we avoid getting all squinky with the retrograde?

First of all check what areas the planet in retrograde deals with and then try not to start any projects that correspond, you can finish things and research things but don't actually start a project. If you do, the likelihood is that you will have to go back and redo it all over again when the retrograde is over.

Be prepared. Two days before the planet stops, either before it goes retrograde or before it goes forward again is when the energies will be at their strongest so batten down the hatches.

Watch out. Twenty-four hours before the planet goes forward again the energies that the planet rules will fling forward like an arrow from a bow.

Not all the retrogrades have noticeable affects on everyday life, those to look out for are Mercury and Mars.

What planets go retrograde and for how long?

Mercury

Time: Goes retrograde three times a year for three weeks each time.

Negative effects: arguments and disagreements, communication problems, travel delays. Electronic and mechanical breakdowns, losing things. Computer problems.

To counteract: read, study, contemplate. Research, tie up loose ends on old projects, always think before you speak. Put the Mercury sign on a yellow candle and ask that the problem slow down and give you time to deal with it.

Venus

Time: Goes retrograde every 18 months and it lasts 40 days.

Negative effects: relationships, money, home decorations.

To counteract: really look at your relationships and how they work. Look for lost items, friends or relatives. Mark a white candle with the Venus symbol, put the candle on top of some money and ask that the spending of it be slowed down and allow you to keep hold of some of your savings.

Mars

Time: Goes retrograde every two years, two months and lasts for 70 days.

Negative effects: aggression, seeing the truth in matters, confusion, karma, anger and resentment.

To counteract: pay off debts, seek closure on old issues, focus on what you want from life, exercise, and clear out clutter.

Jupiter

Time: Goes retrograde once a year for 120 days.

Negative effects: lack of energy, finances if not prepared, generosity, physical problems.

To counteract: work on your inner self. Work with healing energy. Study new subjects.

Saturn

Time: Goes retrograde once a year for 140 days.

Negative effects: rule failure, politics, group structures, delayed or cancelled rewards, abuse.

To counteract: banish negative energies – habits, associations etc. Restructure – yourself, your chores, your household.

Uranus

Time: Goes retrograde once a year for 148 days (the energy is slow and mild).

Negative effects: freedom, humanitarian issues, negative behaviour.

To counteract: direct change, work on the real you.

Neptune

Time: Goes retrograde once a year for 150 days (the energy is slow and mild).

Negative effects: aggressive marketing, the need to escape, drug and alcohol abuse, accusations.

To counteract: unify your groups, meditate, vision quest, all the arts, music and dance, work on the unification of your mind, body and spirit.

Pluto

Time: Goes retrograde once a year for six months.

Negative effects: Not many negative effects, but you might notice people making big changes, getting rid of the old and bringing in the new.

To counteract: Clean everything; throw out old and unwanted junk. Redesign.

Chapter 36

Rites of Passage

Within the pagan world there are several different rites of passage, as there are in many cultures around the world. I would like to share my view of the main ones with you:

Wiccaning/naming ceremony

I held Wiccaning ceremonies for both my children, then naming ceremonies for them both when they were about a year old.

Particularly with my first child I wanted a beautiful blessing as I had a horrible pregnancy and all sorts of complications with the birth, so the beautiful experience I anticipated turned into a bit of a nightmare. The Wiccaning ceremony was in part my way of moving on from the bad experience of the birth.

There are many emotions involved from finding out you are pregnant to giving birth and then a whole heap of new ones while children grow up, some good, some wonderful, some not so good. Celebration of life really starts once a person becomes pregnant, the anticipation and excitement, the planning and preparing both physically and mentally. Rituals and spells can be worked during this time to ask for safe labour, and protection during pregnancy and childbirth.

In the druid tradition new babies that are born are giving a rite of welcoming, often combined with a naming rite at which the child is given a name and where the parents choose guardians or God/Goddess parents, this is when they make their vows to honour and care for the child.

A Wiccaning or naming ceremony can be a private small event with just the parents and the child or a grand affair, or anything in between. Witches and pagans who have Wiccanings for their children use this ceremony to formally announce the child's name to the community to invoke protection for the child and to ask the community to teach the child the values that are important to them. Also at this time deity can be called upon to bless the child.

The most popular age for a Wiccaning seems to be between birth and one year. Although, as I understand it, a Wiccaning can be performed at any age, even adults. Perhaps this could be done if they wish to change their name or at a point of rebirth for themselves.

I don't think it matters where the ritual is held – in a house, in a garden, a field, or the woods – wherever the parents feel comfortable.

Wherever the ritual is to be held the area should be blessed, cleansed and consecrated first. Perhaps request permission from the spirits of the place to accept the ritual and add their energy to it to help make the day run smoothly.

Create a sacred space, maybe decorated with flowers and foliage. Cast the circle, but with the allowance that people and/or children may run or walk in or out, especially if they are not pagan and don't understand circles!

A formal ritual may just include the parents and the child inside, or perhaps a less formal situation with everyone sitting around in a circle. I think it helps to have an altar as a focal point. It doesn't have to be anything grand, but may be decorated with flowers and contain all the tools and essentials for the ritual.

A celebrant leads the ritual, holds the energy and ensures that the ritual flows properly. If you want a less formal event a parent or family member could say the words.

The ceremony can be very flexible. But a basic guideline would be:

Everyone gathers around the circle.

The child and the parents stand at the circle's edge.

The celebrant bids a welcome and gives an outline of what

will happen.

The circle is cast.

The celebrant calls the spirits/elements/guardians/quarters – whatever suits the parent's beliefs.

The circle is cast.

If deities are to be called this would be done too.

The celebrant then speaks a little about the glory of birth, or new life, or the changes that happen within the family. The celebrant might now ask the parents to hold hands and vow their love to each other and their guardianship of the child.

Then the celebrant asks the God/Goddess parents to step forward and make their vow to the child.

Then the child is blessed by the elements, the deities or spirits. Maybe they are even taken to each direction and held up.

The child is then given her name in sight of deity.

Thanks is given to everyone, then the quarters are released, deities thanked and the circle uncast.

I don't believe Wiccanings are historical because 'Wiccan' is a fairly modern term, but I do believe our ancestors held naming ceremonies or blessing ceremonies for new babies. Perhaps this was something simple, such as holding the infant up under the stars and asking blessings from deity.

Menarche (female)

This is the point in life when a girl becomes a lady, when she begins menstruation. I have never seen this part of life as 'a curse' as some call it. Even when I have had bad ones, to me it is a part of the cycle of life; it is part of what makes me a woman.

A girl's menstruation can start as young as 10, it can be as late as 17 or anywhere in between.

Traditionally this was seen as a celebration of life, but in modern times it has become a subject described as a curse or a nuisance.

In Jewish culture the event is still recognised. The Ghanian people celebrate this event with a party; South African Gwi people decorate the young woman with patterns. A girl from the Sioux people would have a purification ritual and guidance from a holy woman. Some cultures involve piercing as part of the ceremony.

The menarche rituals I have researched involve gathering all the women within your community to celebrate, a lot have no men though, or girls who have not begun menstruation yet. They are invited to congratulate the new woman at the end of the ritual and give her gifts.

An idea for this ritual would be to create sacred space. Perhaps have an altar with symbols that are relevant, the Earth, deity statues, pictures of honoured family members and flowers. A flower garland for the girl to wear would be good too.

Cleanse and consecrate the space as you would normally.

The ritual could include dancing and singing to celebrate.

The girl could choose a Moon Mother to attend the ritual with them, to hold her hand and reassure her.

A Moon Father could be chosen to 'crown' the girl after the ceremony with a circlet of flowers.

The girl should be dressed in white and anointed with sacred water, then led into the circle where everyone is already chanting and raising energy. The girl would then turn and call out their name symbolising leaving their girl child behind. Then they would leave the circle and change into a red dress or perhaps just put a red sash on.

Meanwhile all the other women in the circle could pass round a talking stick; as each one receives it they should speak two or three words that summarise their own menarche experience.

The girl re-enters the circle and more singing and celebrating follows.

The Moon Mother would then bless her and perhaps give her a new 'Moon name'.

Then, if men have been excluded, they could join the group and the celebrations. Maybe there would be some storytelling and drumming too.

Coming of age (male)

I believe the coming of age to be very important. It is a time in a lot of cultures when a child becomes an adult. The magical age for boys seems to be 13.

Thirteen is quite a special number, it is a number of transition. 'One' is the individual person starting on the divine path, 'three' is the number of faces of the Goddess (or for Christians the holy trinity). Numerology adds all the numbers together until there is only one, so 1+3=4; four is the number of the whole or the full circle of life.

This age would possibly be a good time to talk to a child about procreation and sexuality. I do believe it is a good idea to be honest and open about such things, rather that a child learns correct details from a parent and be able to ask questions, than they learn the details in the playground!

The Jewish community mark this occasion with a celebration. Native Americans, Africans, aboriginal tribes all mark the occasion of a boy becoming a man. However, it doesn't seem to be something that other communities do in Europe or America from what I can tell. Some cultures involve piercing or tattooing as part of the ceremony.

Perhaps a gift would be nice, some grooming products?

As for a coming of age ceremony I would suggest a similar ritual to that of a Wiccaning.

Handfasting

A handfasting is a pagan 'wedding' based on ancient Celtic traditions.

Historically a handfasting was seen as a rite of betrothal, lasing a year and a day. If the relationship goes well the couple would then hold a second handfasting ceremony that would bind them together as long as their love was shared.

This custom spanned the centuries and was still legal in many parts until 1753 when one Lord Hardwick passed an Act through Parliament declaring that marriages in England could only be legal if sanctioned by the Church. This law, however, was exempt in both Scotland and the Channel Islands. The Act set the precedent for modern Church marriages in the UK ever since, with some updates being allowed for modern times. However, handfastings continued to be legal in Scotland up until 1939, particularly in the Highlands and Islands where they may not have had a permanent clergyman. If this was the case a handfasting ritual could be performed and then when a travelling clergyman visited the community the marriage could then be legalised by the Church. As a direct result of Lord Hardwick's Act and its strict marriage laws, the famous town of Gretna Green became popular with English couples running away to get married because Scotland was outside the jurisdiction of English law.

Handfastings today usually go straight to the second ceremony. A handfasting can last forever, as long as the love is still there, even into future lives.

The setting for most handfastings seems to be outside in a natural place, close to the elements. The space is usually decorated with flowers and foliage. The ceremony is presided over by a priest or priestess whom the couple choose. The space is made sacred and the quarters/elements are called.

The couple are invited into the sacred space to exchange vows with each other. As they give their promises to each other the celebrant binds their wrists together with a cord. This is the actual 'fasting' part signifying their love and knots that indicate their bondage of mutual commitment. This is probably where the saying 'tying the knot' comes from. Rings can also be exchanged at this point. At a lovely handfasting that I had the honour of being a part of recently we used 13 cords, each one a different colour and each to represent a different quality. We had members of the circle bring each cord in one at a time to tie around the wrists of the happy couple.

When the ceremony is over the couple jump the broomstick. This symbolises the joining together of man with woman, to ensure their future happiness and love.

I have read about what was called the 'besom wedding', an unofficial custom that was considered quite lawful in parts of Wales until recent times. A birch besom was placed aslant in the open doorway of the house, with its head on the doorstep and the top of its handle on the door-post. First a young man jumped over it, then his bride, in the presence of witnesses. If either touched or knocked it in any way, the marriage was not recognised. In this kind of marriage, a woman kept her own home and did not become the property of her husband. It was a partnership, 'cyd-fydio,' rather than an ownership. A child of the marriage was considered to be legitimate. If the couple decided to divorce, they simply jumped back over the broomstick again, but this could only be done in the first year of marriage. If a child had come, it was the father's responsibility.

Traditionally the cord used was red in colour, which symbolised desire, vitality and passion of love.

One custom is that while facing each other, the couple place their right hands together and then their left hands together to form an infinity symbol while a cord is tied around their hands in a knot. Another custom is that the man and woman place their right hands only together while a cord is used to tie a knot around their wrists.

In days of old, records were not always kept of who got engaged, married, had children, and died. Today the sacraments of the Church have the responsibility of taking care of these things. Before the Church took over these duties, these things were overseen by the whole community and therefore were set in law by their witnessing what happened between the couple making the promise. If a handfasting was performed with the two left hands together without the tying of the knot, as was the custom of rich and influential German nobility, it meant that the woman was a mistress and would not be able to claim the name, inheritance, property, etc. of the real wife and was only in the protection of the man. But her offspring would be taken care of as legal heirs second in line to the man's legal and first wife. Having lots of children was once the only form of 'Social Security' in one's old age.

Handparting

A handparting is a Pagan divorce, in honour of the fact that sometimes people do grow apart over time.

A handfasting can also be dissolved if things don't work out the way they were intended. Unlike a divorce, they can part easily unless the couple has also chosen to follow the laws of the land and have a registered marriage license and certificate. The binding agreement is between the two parties and the God and Goddess. To undo a handfasting, you must go to the location where it took place (if this is possible). It is not necessary to invite the gathering, just the person who officiated the handfasting and do a reversal on the ceremony, also known as a handparting, to set free each individual from the binding and let each go their separate ways in goodness and love.

A simpler idea is a 'cutting the cords' kind of ceremony, which could be done. Visualize the connections between you, and ask which ones are appropriate for the relationship you wish to have now. Leave those, and cut the others. You might leave a strong connection at the heart and decide to sever the rest at least temporarily, allowing the ones that need to be there for your friendship to grow back.

Croning

I love the idea of a croning ceremony.

The word crone is derived from the word cronus (time) and it means the wisdom gained through life-long experiences. Krone also means crown. To become crowned crone then acknowledges that you are a wise woman who has gathered up the fruits of her experience into profound and sovereign understanding. The wise crone becomes the resource of wisdom for her community and a source of inspiration for her circle of cronies.

A croning ceremony acknowledges the transition into a crone or wise woman, usually when a woman has passed through the menopause. Menopause means the time when menstruation ceases. The last menstruation is a farewell to the motherhood stage of a woman's life. A doorway is now open to step through into the crone phase. Media would have us believe that staying young and firm is what it's all about. And although I am not at the crone stage yet, I do have grey hairs (OK I dye them LOL) and I am starting to get wrinkles, and my body is already fighting against gravity. I am not necessarily happy with all these changes, but I do intend to welcome and celebrate my crone stage when it arrives.

This passage celebrates the end of the time that our energies are turned outwards toward physical activities and marks the beginning of the time that we turn our energies inwards, toward more spiritual activities. Our physical growth slows down, and gradually our physical bodies begin to separate from our spiritual bodies.

In some cultures now and in the past, when a woman had passed the menopause she was considered to keep her wise blood inside her, which increased her wisdom. Elder women were and are still revered and honoured in paganism. A croning ceremony provides acknowledgement and celebration of this.

This can be a personal ceremony, or held with a few close friends or a big celebratory party.

A croning ceremony may include creating sacred space and having all your friends participate. The priest or priestess could say a few words about the person, her qualities and traits. Then each guest could share some memories or mementos.

Then the priest or priestess could say a few words about life and its various stages, how each stage marks changes in our lives and each stage adds to our characters. The person could then be crowned with a circle of flowers.

A presentation of three stones could be made to represent her life – past, present and future.

A candle is lit to represent the light of wisdom, salt is given to represent eternal wisdom and experience. A re-dedication to deity could perhaps take place.

Sagehood

During my research I also discovered a similar ceremony for men who reach 'elderhood' or 'sagehood'. It was also traditional to gift a man his staff on reaching elderhood. It seems the traditional cloak or cape is presented at croning or elderhood.

I also found a lovely idea for the time you reach cronehood or elderhood. Set aside a certain time each week to sit and meditate. For that meditation you take yourself to the world of spirits. A short journey at first to see where it takes you, then each visit you go further and find yourself a home in the spirit world, each future journey you add to it and make it your own. Each week re-examine the details you have made previously and add to it. This meditation creates your very own perfect place ready for when you cross over.

Crossing over

A crossing over or passing over ritual is a way of honouring a departed loved one, of giving blessings and thanks for their lives and honouring their memory. It can also signify aiding their spirit to move on. We all have to pass through the veil at the end of each lifetime. It is this final passage that is celebrated.

Our belief in the Old Religion is in the eternal cycle of birth, death and rebirth. The spirit never dies, but when physical death occurs the spirit moves to another world where it continues to exist until it is reborn again into another physical life.

A ceremony could start with creating sacred space and calling the quarters. Perhaps there could be offerings on the altar for the God and Goddess of the Underworld and a candle on the altar to represent the spirit of that person, lit at the beginning of the ritual.

The priest or priestess could say a few words about the person who has passed over to honour their memory, maybe going around the circle and asking each person to add a few words too. As each person says their words they could sprinkle some flower petals into a cauldron filled with water in the centre of the circle.

The priest or priestess would then ask all the elements to guide the person on their journey. Then deity would be asked to guide the person to the Summerlands and protect them.

When the priest or priestess feels the loved one has departed, they would snuff out the candle. They could then wrap the candle in silk, spoon some of the water and petals from the cauldron into a holder and present both items to the person who requested the ritual for their loved one. Although sometimes it is preferred the candle should be left to burn out on its own.

A memorial rite can also be performed after a 'mainstream' funeral. This ritual calls upon the deceased in order to complete any unfinished business in the material world, and to bid a final farewell before sending the spirit to Summerland.

Chapter 37

The Summerlands

Generally witches believe in reincarnation and that when we die we go to the Summerlands. Now this is a bit of a generalisation, but I will share my thoughts with you.

Do you ever get that feeling that you are remembering something rather than learning it? I have done that a lot within the Craft, and I firmly believe that it is because I have lived before, many lifetimes in fact. I also know that some of my friends and sisters and brothers within the Craft and myself have met before in other lifetimes, it's that feeling of familiarity when you meet someone new.

The Otherworld, the Summerlands or the Isle of Avalon. I have also heard it called Tir Na N'og. I do believe that it will appear to each person differently. However we perceive the Otherworld will be how it manifests to us. I don't personally believe in a hell, I do believe that each soul has been on the planet to learn, to grow – if that person has done something terrible in life they will move on from that once they reach the Otherworld.

To me the Otherworld is where our spirit, our essence, goes once we die. To me it is the Isle of Avalon. The spirit exists there in harmony with others, spirits we have known in the life we have just left and those that we may have known in past lives. Then when the time is right, when there is a suitable 'new life' ready for us, we live again to learn a new lesson. We have to go through these different lives to learn and grow.

The idea of the Isle of Avalon as the Otherworld makes perfect sense to me. A trip in a small wooden boat, paddled by a dark cloaked ferryman across the water to the magical isle to meet my ancestors suits me fine. But as I say, everyone will see it differently.

Chapter 38

A Bit of Hoodoo

Now I bet you are all thinking, 'Eeek I don't want anything to do with the Voodoo black magic stuff,' and I promise it isn't!

Voodoo or Voudoun is a religion and it has been given a lot of bad press by Hollywood. However, we aren't going to deal with that. What we are going to look at is the magical practice called hoodoo.

Now obviously I am not a born and bred hoodoo priestess, but I have done a lot of study on the art of hoodoo and I use it a lot in my spell and craft work, it is a fascinating area of magic and I think it reflects a lot in the traditional English folk magic.

Hoodoo is a magic tradition that is a pick-and-mix blend of African tradition, Native American medicine, Judeo-Christian ritual and European folk magic. Although its roots can be traced back to Africa it seems to have been established during the time of slavery in the USA and it does seem to now generally be an American tradition. Although I don't believe that it is actually referred to as 'hoodoo' in the households it is practised in. It seems to be a collective word that the media have come up with, but it seems to have been adopted so we shall use it.

So what actually is hoodoo?

Hoodoo is a magical practice, the primary function being healing using herbs, plants, roots, trees, animals, minerals and natural waters, using them alongside amulets, chants, rituals and power objects. It is natural and practical. It covers the blessing of homes, peaceful environments and keeping out unwanted spirits. It also deals with love, relationships, health, happiness, luck, fortune and success, but it does also cover binding, hexing and unhexing.

An important part of working hoodoo is the 'laying of tricks' and 'fixing tricks'. These are very similar to gypsy magic workings and folk magic. The most common item used is a small bag filled with herbs and magical items – known as a mojo bag, a gris gris or a nation sack.

I do want to talk a bit about the word 'mojo' here, for those of you that have seen any of the Austin Powers films where he uses the word mojo as a sexual reference, this is NOT what mojo means. Mojo is more about spirit and power. A mojo bag is essentially an amulet used for various intents. The bag is usually carried close on your person. If someone 'steals your mojo' what they have actually done is stolen your amulet bag, thus taking away your hopes and dreams with it. A mojo bag is a very personal item, it carries with it your own personal energy so it is very precious and you do not want it falling into the hands of another.

Hoodoo also uses a lot of magical oils and incenses. These can be used on your body, in burners, around the home or to dress candles. Hoodoo also uses salts, magic powders and sweet waters for spiritual cleansing, bathing the body, left around the home and in workings.

Divination in hoodoo incorporates the use of natural items such as bones, crystals, stones, shells, and twigs along with tea leaf and coffee ground reading, water scrying and crystal gazing.

In hoodoo you use the energies of ancestral and nature spirits for protection, divination, healing, and blessings and if you choose to use them… curses.

Hoodoo is also a HUGE subject with a lot of spiritual diversities and connections, hopefully what I have included in this book will give you a taster to research more.

Roots

Rootwork is another name for hoodoo; it is about understanding and working with herbalism and nature.

Roots are an important ingredient in hoodoo. The root of a

plant contains a lot of good energy, and they are the source of life for the plant itself. If we use the root in a working we are essentially tapping into that life source of energy. Although we must be mindful here, if you take the roots of a plant, it is not likely to grow back so use it sparingly.

Trees

Trees play a big part in hoodoo; a good hoodoo practitioner will know everything there is to know about trees and their magical uses. They will know and understand the mysteries and secrets that the trees have to share with us. The bark, wood, leaves and flowers are all used in hoodoo.

Part of hoodoo practice is called 'sticking'. This is a way of piercing something. You might think about 'sticking' performed on a poppet, but it also covers sticking thread into a piece of fabric or sticking by magic until it works.

Stones

Stones are also used. They hold huge amounts of energy and history. Think how long a stone or pebble has been around. Any stones you use in hoodoo will need to be charged as you would in most magic, by leaving them out in the sun or moonlight, soaked in special waters or anointed with oils or in salt.

Metals

Another important part of hoodoo is to use metals – silver, copper, brass, iron, lead and lodestone. They all have their own individual magical properties and can be used as you would crystals.

Silver: represents the sea, the Goddess and the Moon. Helps with intuition, dreams, fertility and love.

Copper: used for healing and a good conduit for spiritual healing energy. Works well when combined with quartz crystals. Copper pennies are used in hoodoo charms for luck and money magic.

Brass: used in place of gold as it has all the magical properties but no vanity. Good for love magic.

Iron: represents one of the Orisha deities Ogun, a warrior and protector. Nails are used a lot in hoodoo workings.

Lead: holds and delivers intent. You can use a simple lead pencil when writing out spells to symbolise the power of lead, although most modern pencils no longer have real lead in them.

Lodestone: for love, luck and prosperity. Fool's gold and pyrite are also used.

Ashe

Ashe is nature; it is the invisible power that is nature herself. Ashe is in all natural things – plants, stones, herbs and anything that you make from them such as herbal teas, spiritual washes, charms, and soaps. Even your magical words contain Ashe.

Chapter 39

Feathers, Bones, Shells and Eggs

Feathers

I work a lot with feathers in my magic, maybe because I seem to find so many of them!

Feathers are symbolic of the element of air and also carry with them the magical energies of the bird that they came from. A lot of bird totems are also air spirits or faeries. They use the bird to connect directly with us. The use of feathers in workings and meditations can help us make that connection, to tap into that energy.

Dem bones

In the old days bones and animal parts were used widely for magical purposes. People were hunters; they used all the parts of an animal primarily for food and warmth, and the bones for magic. In hoodoo especially they use a lot of chicken blood and bones. If you are squeamish – it's OK you don't have to use them!

Now I do not advocate anyone popping out and hitting a squirrel over the head with a stick just to use the bones in a spell. However, nature itself provides dead animals and birds and man in his motor car provide a lot too. Picking up road kill may sound a bit yucky and is not for everyone or the faint hearted (thankfully I have a good friend who is very brave and does it for me), but I think of it as honouring the animal, that its skin and bones will be put to some good use after it has passed away. Don't forget that you will also get bones from your roast chicken dinner…

Bones are to me a sort of fetish. The word fetish originates from a Portuguese word meaning charm or sorcery, an item filled with magic. Feathers, leaves, twigs and stones are all also types of fetish.

The bones themselves are a good way of connecting with the spirit of the animal and working with those energies. The bone of an animal works as a vessel for the spirit to reside in within our realm. Animal bones can also be carried in medicine bags to utilise their particular energies. All animal spirits take time to bond with, so don't rush it and it is also a nice idea to leave offerings for the animal bones too.

You can wear the bones as well to take on the attributes and power of the animal that they belonged to. A lot of animals are shamanic in nature too, enabling you to tap into their ability to travel between worlds.

Feathers, animal skins or bones can also be used in shapeshifting. The skins can be worn, the feathers or bones used as jewellery to aid you in taking on the form of the animal.

Ritual tools can also be made from animal bones – rattles for instance – or tie bones to your staff or wand for an added energy boost.

Divination with animal bones can also be done.

The magic of sea shells

Living near the sea I am lucky enough to be able to collect sea shells easily, I love walking along the beach and always come back with pockets full of shells and hag stones.

So how about the magical properties of the humble sea shell?

Obviously sea shells are associated with water. I often use a shell to represent west when I am in ritual, and I also use them in water element witches bottles.

The Moon controls the tides of the ocean so shells are also associated with the Moon. I have a large round flat mother of pearl shell on my main altar to represent the Moon.

Being associated with water and the Moon I think the shell works perfectly in spells for emotions too.

Shells also have an association with Aphrodite, so can also be used for love spells. Use a shell as a love drawing talisman.

In the past shells were also used in some parts of the world as currency, so they also have the association of money and prosperity. Use in money drawing medicine bags or pop a small shell in your purse.

Think about what a shell is, it is a protective covering for the creature inside, making shells also good for protection. Use them in your witch's bottles, or strung on a necklace for this purpose.

Particular shells also have their own individual meanings:

Abalone: general use and containment of empowered herbs and stones
Clam: purification and love
Conche: love
Cone shell: protection
Cowrie: prosperity, money – if you look at a cowrie shell is also looks very 'feminine' ;-) in hoodoo this shell is also used for purity, cleansing and new beginnings
Whelk: dramatic positive change
Limpet: courage, confidence, strength
Scallop: travel, movement

If you are collecting your own shells please make sure that the creature is not still inside it. If you do pick up one with a living creature toss it back into the water.

If you are purchasing shells in a shop or from the internet please make sure they are from sustainable and viable sources.

Magical eggs

Eggs symbolise the essence of life, rebirth and fertility. Within that they also symbolise long life and also immortality. An egg itself encompasses the mystery and magic of creation.

In legend faeries would consume eggs of mythical birds such as the phoenix.

Throughout history people have eaten eggs for lots of different reasons, some to absorb the magical properties by eating them, others to ensure fertility.

In the Slavonic and Germanic lands people also smeared eggs onto their hoes to ensure fertility for the soil. In Iran brides and grooms exchange eggs for fertility. In 17th century France, a bride would break an egg when she entered her new home for the first time.

The idea that eggs were a symbol of fertility and life force compelled certain cultures not only to shun them as food but also to avoid destroying them at all costs.

Certain aboriginal groups in Australia believed they descended from the emu, so strict taboos were placed on eating the eggs of these ancestral birds.

Eggs were often used for divination. This stemmed from the belief that eggs symbolised life and particularly life in the future. One method involved painting the eggs, boiling them and reading the patterns in their cracks. Another method involved tossing the eggs and divining the future, a system of divination known as oomancy. Egg white can also be used, by dripping it into a bowl of water and reading the shapes that it makes.

In Egypt eggs were hung in the temples to bring fertility, for birth and renewal. The Hindu description of the beginning of the world saw it as a cosmic egg.

The yolk in the centre of the egg has also been used to represent the Sun.

Cascarilla is made from egg shells that have been crushed and ground to a powder. It is used in hoodoo and folk magic as well as other magical practices. The powder can be dusted on the body to protect from spirit possession and also acts as a shield from psychic or magical attack. It can be sprinkled around the perimeter of your home to create a peaceful environment and to protect from intruders. It can also be used for drawing runes, sigils or other symbols in rituals and workings.

The egg is a complete set of elements in one handy pack: the shell represents earth, the inner membrane represents air, the yolk is fire and the white is water.

Chapter 40

Poppets, Medicine Bags, Powders, Smudges and Washes

Poppets

I regularly use poppets in my spell work. They are easy to make and work exceptionally well. Forget the media view that poppets are evil and the work of dark voodoo priests, it is a load of old hooey! Poppets have been used for thousands of years, going right back to Egyptian times and originally they were used for healing.

I like to use felt to make the base poppet because I am lazy at sewing and felt doesn't need hemming. I also use it because it is easily available in all sorts of colours, so you can add a bit of colour magic to your poppet.

Use a simple shape for your poppet. I like to use a 'gingerbread man' shape or sometimes just a 'T' shape, it depends how artistic and creative you are.

Sew a button on for one eye and embroider the other eye, or just embroider both eyes, add a mouth and a heart and the poppet starts to take shape.

I fill the poppet with a little bit of stuffing to bulk it out and then fill the rest with a herb blend that corresponds with my intent, charging the herbs as I add them.

Then I sew up the poppet and charge him again with my intent. Sometimes I add wool for hair, sometimes I wrap small strips of cloth around its middle so that petitions can be written on slips of paper and tucked into the cloth bands. You can also pop a small crystal inside your poppet too.

The poppet can then be put on an altar to work its magic. Hoodoo practitioners tend to bury the poppet in the earth for the spell to work.

Poppet stuffing recipes

Healing: lemon balm, carnation flowers, rosemary, thyme, ivy
Prosperity: mint, basil, honeysuckle flowers, poppy seeds
Success: lemon balm, cinnamon, rowan, sage
Happiness: marjoram, meadowsweet, lavender
Protection: peppercorns, rosemary, sage, bay, juniper, salt, ivy
Love: lemon balm, cinnamon, thyme, rose petals, lavender, geranium petals
Psychic abilities: marigold flowers, thyme, bay, rose petals, rowan

Medicine bags

A medicine bag contains items that are charged with your intent and each item is a guide for the spirits to help them understand what the outcome you desire is. Your medicine bag, once it is put together, is essentially 'alive' with energy and it will need to be looked after and 'fed' with magic powder. You will need to feed it periodically to maintain its energy force.

Africans call the power of nature 'ashe' and this is what is present in all herbs, plants, stones, in fact anything from nature. It is this power that we are using within the medicine bags.

A medicine bag can contain all sorts of items – herbs, roots, spices, crystals, feathers, bones, shells, dirt, pebbles, coins – what you put in your medicine bag is up to you.

Make up a little bag from material scraps, or felt (as it won't fray) or you can use the wedding favour bags available from craft shops. The colour is up to you. In hoodoo a medicine bag is usually made from red flannel, but I like to tie in colour magic and use material the colour of the intent that the bag is for.

Charge each item with your intent as you put it in the bag.

Fast luck

Use green material for the bag and add:

Feathers
Nutmeg – for luck
A red lodestone
Six silver coins

Stay away

Use orange or black material for the bag and add:

Rosemary
Pinch of dirt (graveyard dirt is good for this)
Pinch of dried dragon's blood (a plant resin)
A black onyx

Love drawing

Use red or pink material for the bag and add:

Rose petals
Lemon balm
Stick of cinnamon
Rose quartz
A sea shell

Money draw

Use green material for the bag and add:

Mint
Honeysuckle flowers
Three poppy seed heads
A piece of malachite
A silver coin

Good health

Use blue material for the bag and add:

Carnation flower heads
Rosemary
Thyme
A piece of willow
A piece of string tied with three knots, for health, healing and strength

Magic powders

Now to make the powder to feed your medicine bag, although magic powders also have lots of other uses. They can be used to roll candles in for spell work, to sprinkle around your house for protection, to add oomph to rituals and any spells, to add to poppets and witches bottles or to wear in a small bottle as a charm.

To make a magic powder the ingredients you use must be ground so you will need either a pestle and mortar or the end of a rolling pin and a solid bowl.

As you add each ingredient to the bowl charge it first with your intent. I also like to charge the powder as a whole once it is complete too.

This can then be fed to your medicine bag each week, just a sprinkle; you can even boost the power by feeding it on the corresponding day of the week to your intent. Or keep it in an airtight bottle or jar and use it for all sorts of other spell work.

I like to use a base for my magic powders. I usually use either salt or sugar, which grind well and add their own qualities to the mix too. If I am making faerie wishes powder I also like to add in a little bit of glitter!

The recipes below don't have measurements as it depends how much you want to make of each one and it allows you to experiment and go with your instincts.

Fast luck powder

Ground nutmeg

Ground cinnamon
Sugar for sweet success
Lemon balm

Stay away powder

Mustard powder
Salt
Rosemary
Garlic powder

Love drawing powder

Lavender
Ginger
Marjoram
Sugar

Money drawing powder

Sugar
Poppy seeds
Mint
Cloves

Health and healing powder

Salt
Lemon balm
Rosemary
Thyme

Spiritual washes and smudges

You and your home can attract all sorts of energies and vibrations, so I think it is good practise to routinely have a spiritual clear out every so often.

It isn't just the magic that you work within your home that will bring in energies, everything that comes from outside will bring its own energies with it. For instance, your grocery shopping will have been held and touched by many people, each one adding their own energies to it, and they won't always be good energies.

Salt is particularly good for spiritual house cleaning. Sprinkle a little in the corners of each room for purification and protection.

Smudging – this can be done with a bunch of dried sage, dried rosemary, dried lavender, sweet grass (or a combination) or even with your favourite incense. You can either start at your front door or in the centre of your home, but work your way around your house, going into each room and wafting the smoke around, making sure it gets into all the corners. You can use a chant whilst you are doing this, asking any negative energy to leave and to be replaced with positive, loving and happy energy.

You can clean out the negative energy by sweeping with a besom, sweeping from the front of the house to the back and sending out any negativity. You can even add a few drops of essential oil to the bristles of your broom to help.

You can make your own cleansing and purifying mist using a spray bottle filled with distilled or sterilised water (or boil the water in your kettle and let it cool), adding a few drops of essential oil to it and popping a rosemary, sage or lavender sprig into the bottle. Rose water, frankincense, cinnamon and lavender are all good for this purpose.

Chase away spray

250ml distilled water
9 drops frankincense essential oil
9 drops myrrh essential oil
3 drops rosemary essential oil

Spiritual uplift spray

250ml distilled water

6 drops bergamot essential oil
9 drops lemon essential oil
9 drops grapefruit essential oil
3 drops rose essential oil

Peace and harmony spray

250ml distilled water
6 drops bergamot essential oil
9 drops rosewood essential oil
6 drops juniper essential oil

Hearts and kisses spray

250 ml distilled water
9 drops patchouli essential oil
3 drops cardamom essential oil
9 drops ylang ylang essential oil
6 drops mandarin essential oil

Once you have done the general housework you can use spiritual cleansers such as floor washes. These washes can also be used on worktops too.

All-purpose floor wash

6 drops rosemary essential oil
6 drops pine needle essential oil
You can also add geranium or orange oil to give it a bit of spiritual uplift too.
Add the wash to your bucket of water and start mopping!

Spiritual cleansing of you

Don't forget you! We can also pick up bad energies or negativity on our body too, so it pays to spiritually cleanse.

In the bath tub

You can add all sorts of herbs and oils to your bath tub along with burning scented candles or incense while you bathe.

Lavender, patchouli and frankincense are all good oils to use. You can also make herbal tea bags to put in the water too. Add a combination of dried herbs and spices to a square of muslin, tie it with ribbon and either hang it under the tap in the running water or pop it in the tub.

Bath salts

These are incredibly easy to make if you prefer to use them. Mix together:

2 cups (16oz) sea salt
1 cup (8oz) Epsom salt
6 drops essential oil of your choice
1 teaspoon of herbs or flower petals

This makes a large amount of bath salts, you will only need one tablespoon of it for each bath. Write yourself a cleansing and purifying chant to say whilst you are soaking in the water.

Body powders

Body powders are easy to make too, much like magic powders but for our body! Mix together:

2 tablespoons baking soda
5 tablespoons arrowroot or cornstarch
6 teaspoons of powdered herbs and/or flower petals
12 drops essential oil

These powders can be made for specific intents, to improve the spirits you might use lavender, rose petals and orange (powdered dried orange peel works very well).

Body mists

Body mists are also easy to make, as with the room mists, same principle – fill a mister bottle with distilled water and add your own herbs and essential oils. For de-stressing your might use rose, orange, geranium and lavender.

Perfume

Making your own perfume is so easy, use a base of distilled water and vodka and add essential oil. You can leave out the alcohol but it won't keep for as long. Mix together:

16 drops of essential oil of your choice
8 ozs distilled water
4 tablespoons vodka

Leave out the vodka and you can also use this recipe to make anointing oil.

Chapter 41

Offerings

Offerings can be made up from hand blended natural herbs and spices. These can be sprinkled on the ground under your favourite tree, in your garden, in the sea – wherever you feel works the best for your intent. Or you can burn them as incense. They can also be kept with you in a bag or pocket or placed on your altar. Offerings sometimes include small crystals too.

I have two offering dishes on my main altar, one for the God and one for the Goddess – all sorts of things find their way into those offering bowls depending on what I feel is needed. They even like chocolate on occasion.

All the ingredients should correspond to the deity or element you wish to honour. If your offering has an intent with it too, such as love or prosperity, tie the ingredients into that too.

If you were making an offering to a deity you should check what herbs or flowers correspond to them, or better still meditate for a while and decide what YOU think they would like.

You can be adventurous with offerings. For instance if you were making an offering to an Orisha, he might like tobacco in there too.

If the offering is for the fae, then they love honey and flower petals, so those could be added to your ingredients.

This is all about deciding what your intended recipient likes. What does the deity you wish to offer like? What would make them happy? For instance, what ingredients really say air to you if you are offering to the air elemental?

Make the offering personal. But if you are intending to leave the offering outside for nature, please make sure none of it is toxic and all of it is biodegradable.

Chapter 42

Oils

Oil blends are useful for dressing candles for spell work, adding to your own bath water for a ritual bath or using to anoint yourself before ritual. Please test a drop or two on a small area of your skin before you go slapping on loads of oil, just in case you are allergic to it.

Oil blends are easy to make, and you can use any type of base oil such as almond oil, jojoba oil, apricot kernel oil, coconut oil, even olive oil, then add a few drops of essential oil in whatever blends you want. Tie them into your intent or correspond them to an element or deity. Play around, experiment with blends and have fun with it. If you are experimenting with blends I would suggest using pieces of card to test the blends on first. Put a drop of each essential oil on a small slip of card (or paper towel) add the next oil and sniff to see if you like it, then add the next drop etc. Make up several different blends on slips of cards to decide what scents work together. This way you won't end up ruining a whole bottle of base oil by adding in random essential oils.

Unhex oil

10ml base oil
9 drops black pepper essential oil
3 drops vertiver essential oil
9 drops ginger essential oil

Soul heal oil

10ml base oil
9 drops geranium essential oil
9 drops palmarosa essential oil
3 drops lime essential oil

Dragon oil

10ml base oil
13 drops dragon's blood essential oil
9 drops nutmeg essential oil
9 drops patchouli essential oil

Blessing oil

10ml base oil
6 drops lavender essential oil
3 drops rosemary essential oil
6 drops juniper essential oil
6 drops rose essential oil

Spiritual cleansing oil

10ml base oil
9 drops sandalwood essential oil
9 drops patchouli essential oil
3 drops geranium essential oil

Chapter 43

Witch Bottles and Ladders

I love using witch bottles, I always have two on the go in my house for protection, clearing out negative energies and bringing happiness to the home.

These are so easy to make, you don't need special pretty bottles you can just use old clean jam jars.

The basic structure of a witch bottles can be used for any purpose, protection, for financial gain, for helping with artistic creativity, to call forth positive energy (instead of 'just filtering out negative energy'), for improving health, etc.

Basically a witch bottle is a container of some sort, usually a jar or a bottle, which is filled with objects that have a given magical purpose. The person making the witch bottle, or in other words the one casting the bottled spell, can charge the objects magically beforehand and build the bottle to work on this charging until the need for renewing the spell arises. Witch bottles can also be built to recharge themselves by the energy they 'capture' for as long as the bottle stays unbroken, whether it is years or centuries.

The typical contents of the basic protective witch bottle today are quite similar to that of the traditional one: nails, sand or different coloured sands, crystals, stones, knotted threads, herbs, spices, resin, flowers, candle wax, incense, votive candles, salt, vinegar, oil, coins, saw dust, ashes etc. Actually, everything used in 'normal spells' can be used in this bottled version of a spell, the witch bottle.

Original witch bottles were used to keep witches away. They also used to contain all sorts of bodily fluids, hair and finger nail clippings – you can still use these if you wish.

Basically start with your jar or bottle, then charge each item before you add it, layering up the 'ingredients' as you go.

It really is up to you what you put in. I like to put in three nails to attract negativity and for protection, I also put in a piece of string with three knots in, knotting in my intent with each tie. If it is for prosperity I often drop in a silver coin. I usually put salt in for protection, cleansing and purification. I also like to add some kind of dried pulses – lentils or beans to 'soak' up any negative energy. Garlic is good for protection too. Then add any herbs, spices and flowers that correspond with your intent – rose petals for love, cinnamon for success, mint and basil for prosperity etc. Keep filling the jar or bottle up until you reach the top then put the lid on. If you are using a jam jar I like to draw a pentacle on the lid. If you are using a bottle with a cork I like to seal the cork lid with dripped wax.

If I am making the witch bottle for protection for my own home I like to put in a pebble from the garden, a couple of fallen leaves from the tree in my yard and a bit of cobweb from inside the house, it makes it all more personal and ties the bottle to the energies of the home.

Money jar

A twist on the witch bottle is a money jar.

Use a clean, cleansed jar and half fill it with rice or seeds (fenugreek seeds are good). As you half fill the jar visualise prosperity and abundance. Then every day add two more seeds to the jar, visualising prosperity as you do. When the jar is full bury the seeds whilst sending up a request to deity that your desire will be fulfilled.

You can also do this with a jar and your loose change. Each time you drop a couple of coins in the jar visualise prosperity, every so often sprinkle in a few herbs that correspond with prosperity such as basil or mint. When the jar is full you can count it up and use it for something special.

War bottle

A hoodoo war water bottle would be sent, left on your doorstep or thrown at an enemy. Each bottle contained, basically, a swampy or bloody yuck, which if thrown at your property would smash and leave a foul smelling mess. It has been said that to break a bottle of war water on the property of your enemy will bring strife and sorrow to their household. I would imagine that just the mess would be enough!

War water bottles may have contained such items as black feathers, blood (probably from chickens) or blood substitutes (beetroot or tomato juice for instance), moss, rusty nails and broken glass among other things.

Each item was symbolic – the nails were to tie down wayward spirits, broken glass suggested the transparent spirit world and they all came together to give the warning.

However, there is another use for these bottles in African American tradition and that is to use as a trap for wayward spirits.

I took the basic war bottle idea and kitchen witchified it (if that is even a word) and came up with the Dark World Bottle.

The contents of the Dark World Bottle are 'swamp inspired' and used as a trap for wayward spirits, bad thoughts and negative vibes.

Use this bottle to trap and ensnare bad and negative energies, dark thoughts, moods and feelings and any nasty vibes. Once you feel it is full take the bottle to a safe place and smash it – sending its contents back to Mother Earth to be purified, taking with it any leftover nasties. Ahhhh... feel the beautiful release!!

But, please be careful to clear up any broken glass and dispose of it safely.

Dark World Bottle

Soil
Beetroot juice

Marigold flowers
Carnation flowers
Peppercorns
Dried chillies
Star anise
Rice
Rowan
Black salt
Sand
Juniper berries

Witches' ladders

In 1886, while repairing an old house in Somerset, England, in the roof was found what is now considered the first recorded find of a witch's ladder. It was a length of braided cord with a loop at one end and lots of cockerel feathers threaded through.

Many people have theorised over the years as to the purpose of witches' ladders, ranging from stealing milk from a neighbour's cow to the curse of death, but also covering healing and to bring wishes. There doesn't appear to be any actual evidence of what they were for or that they were even used by witches, but I think the idea works very well.

The basic structure is that of braiding three, nine or 12 cords together. They can be made from string, ribbon or twine. The idea is to weave your spell into the cords as you plait, chanting as you go if you wish. Colour magic can be added in if you want to, with the use of coloured ribbon, beads or feathers. Charms, buttons and bells can also be added in. Once your plait is done, you can pop feathers or sprigs of herbs in between the threads to add intent to your spell.

Chapter 44

Celebrating the Sabbats

This section goes into detail about how I celebrate the Sabbats, it also gives ideas on correspondences, spells, oil and incense ingredients, meditations and a whole heap of craft ideas for each celebration. For each of the incense and oil recipes I have purposely not given measurements, as a general rule it is equal amounts of each, but experiment and see what works for you.

Autumn Equinox

20th – 22nd September

Mabon (pronounced may-bun or may-bon)

This is the second harvest, where our ancestors would have been storing away food to last the cold winter months.

This is the time of year when we give thanks to the Sun and all that it has helped provide for us as we welcome in the dark half of the year. It is a kind of bitter sweet time of the year really, but also one of my favourite times. Although we still get warm, sunny days, there is the feel of autumn in the air, the mornings and evenings have that crisp, fresh feel to them.

Take some time to think about what you want to achieve in the next few months, make plans and start a new project that you can work on over the winter months.

Symbols

Squashes, gourds, pine cones, acorns, grain, vines, apples, pomegranates, seeds, cornucopias and sun wheels.

In the garden

In my garden the rosemary will still be going strong as will the thyme and bay, but the other herbs such as marjoram/oregano will be starting to fade now. Dahlias, asters and chrysanthemums will be flowering, but most of the other bedding plants will be past their best. Time to start tidying up and cutting back.

Herbs

Yarrow, rosemary, marigold, sage, frankincense, rose hips, sunflower, oak and apple.

Foods

Bread, nuts, apples, pomegranates, root vegetables, grapes, cinnamon, cloves, nutmeg, oak leaves and grapes.

Colours

Red, orange, brown, gold, royal blue, burgundy and dark green.

Activities

Wine making, harvesting and drying the last of the herbs, seeds and flower petals. Make offerings to trees and plants. Take walks in the woods to begin to see the coming of autumn. Make soup stocks and jams.

Crafts

God's Eye

These are really easy to make and you can create them in any colour or colours. For Mabon it is good to use autumnal colours though. What you need:

> Two sticks of equal length, you could use dowel rod, lolly sticks, twigs, cinnamon sticks or even wooden skewers.
> Wool, yarn, string or ribbon in whatever colours you choose
> Feathers, shells, beads etc if you want to add them in.

As you make the eye work some magic into it, visualise your

intent as you wrap the yarn. You could work in protection for your home, love, peace or prosperity.

First you make the two sticks into a cross, lay them one across the other equally then wrap your wool around the top arm of the cross once or twice where the two sticks meet, working widdershins as you come round on the left side of the upper arm, cross down and over to the bottom side of the right arm. Bring the wool out behind the top of the right arm and cross over to the left side of the bottom arm. Lastly bring the wool from the right side of the bottom arm across to the top side of the left arm. (Don't forget to hold the loose end of the wool in place and wrap the wool over it to keep it from unravelling.)

It sounds complicated but once you get going with it, it will all make sense.

Continue wrapping the sticks following the same order until you have the amount of colour you want, then you can switch to a different colour and continue, repeat this until you have used all the colours you wish to and it is the size you want. Finish by making a loop with wool so that you can hang it up.

You can also decorate the ends of the sticks with beads, crystals, feathers, ribbons, anything you fancy really. You could also sew some charms onto the God's Eye itself if you wanted to.

Hang the God's Eye above your altar or on a wall to celebrate the Sabbat.

Apple candle holders

I always have several candles on my altar whatever the season is, apples are good to use as holders at this time of the year.

What you need:

Firm apples or even small squashes
Lemon juice
Herbs of your choice
Taper candles

Rinse the fruit or vegetable and dry. Give the outside a bit of a polish to make it clean and shiny. Using a knife or a corer, make a hole in the top where the stem is. Work down about halfway into the fruit so that the candle will have a firm base. Make the hole the same diameter as your candle.

Pour some lemon juice into the hole and let it sit for a few minutes, this helps to stop the fruit from going brown and squishy too quickly. Pour out the lemon juice and then dry the inside.

Insert a sprig of fresh herbs into the hole, rosemary or thyme works well. Then add take your taper candle and drip a small amount of wax into the hole to secure the candle and quickly set the candle in to it.

Drying apples

I love drying apple slices, it fills the whole house with the most amazing scent. What you need:

Apples (obviously)
Lemon juice
Salt
Ground spices – cinnamon, clove, nutmeg, cardamom or a mixture of your choice

Slice up your apple or apples horizontally so that the star shape shows in the centre, make them just under ¼ inch thick. Place the slices in a bowl and sprinkle with a little lemon juice, give them a gentle stir so that they are all coated. Then take them out and dry them with paper towels.

Next, sprinkle the apple slices on both sides with your spice mixture.

Now the next step is your choice, you can either string the apple slices onto some twine and leave them hanging in a dry place, they will take a couple of weeks to dry, or you can lay the slices on baking sheets and dry them in the oven on a really, really low heat, this takes four to six hours.

Once dried, the slices will feel a bit rubbery but they will last for ages and ages. They can be made into wreaths, used in incense or pot pourri.

Apple wreath

Using the dried apple slices you can make a wreath. What you need:

- Plenty of apple slices
- Wire, this can be florist wire, craft wire or even an old coat hanger

Bend the wire into a circle, a square, a heart – whatever shape you want your wreath to be, then thread the dried apple slices onto it until it is full. Finally fix the ends together with pliers then add some ribbon in a loop to hang the wreath from.

Wreath of leaves

This is an easy and simple wreath to make. What you need:

- Artificial leaves from the craft store or real autumn leaves
- Paper plate or thick cardboard
- Raffia or ribbon
- Glue
- Scissors

Cut a hole in the middle of the paper plate to make it wreath shaped (or cut a wreath shape from cardboard), make small hole in one edge and thread your ribbon or raffia through it and make a loop to hang it up with.

Glue your leaves onto the paper wreath shape, covering it completely.

You can add silk flowers, glitter or sequins too.

Pine cone bird feeder

Birds love these! They like the tiny seeds that lie within the pinecones and peanut butter is an excellent source of fat and protein for wild birds.

What you need:

Pine cones
Peanut butter
Birdseed
String or wire

Tie the string at the top of the pine cone so that you can hang it in a tree. Using a knife, push the peanut butter into all the little openings on the pinecone. Then roll the pinecone in the birdseed, press the seeds in as much as you can.

Hang the feeder in your garden.

Leaf garland

Easy to make and so pretty. What you need:

Fabric scraps or wrapping paper in autumn colours or real leaves
Cord, string or ribbon
Scissors
Glue
Card

If you are using fabric or paper you will need to cut out leaf shapes and then glue them onto card to make them stiff enough.

Take your leaf shapes or your real leaves and carefully make a small hole in each (a hole punch is useful) then string them onto your cord or ribbon until you have the length of garland you require.

Incense

Frankincense, sandalwood, juniper, pine, oak, marigold, sandalwood, rosehip

Autumn Equinox incense recipe

Frankincense
Juniper
Sandalwood
Pine
Rosehip

Blend them all together.

Oils

Patchouli, cinnamon, pine, sage, apple, rosemary, frankincense, chamomile

Autumn Equinox oil recipe

Blend together the following essential oils, with a base oil:

Rosemary
Frankincense
Apple
Chamomile

Autumn Equinox oil recipe 2

Blend together the following essential oils, with a base oil:

Walnut
Almond
Marigold leaves

Spell workings

The Autumn Equinox is a good time to work spells for protection, prosperity, security, harmony, balance and self confidence.

Prosperity candle spell

What you need:

A green, gold or brown candle – use a small candle so that it doesn't take days to burn!
Essential oil – your choice, but basil or pine is good for prosperity.
Herbs of your choice – but again basil and pine are good for prosperity and poppy seeds are good for money
A small knife or pin
Slip of paper
Pen
Cauldron or fire proof dish

Take your candle and carve symbols into it that represent prosperity to you. It could be a pound or a dollar sign, it could be a rune or a sigil – go with what works for you.

Then dress the candle with essential oil, work from the centre of the candle up to the top and from the centre down to the bottom, as you dress the candle charge it with your intent.

Then write down your desire for prosperity, abundance, money needed – whatever your particular requirement is – on the slip of paper. As you write visualise yourself receiving it.

Sprinkle the herbs on to the candle and then light it. Spend some time visualising your needs being met.

Once you have the visualisation set in your mind take the slip of paper and carefully light it in the flame of the candle and drop it into your cauldron or fireproof dish.

Allow the slip of paper and the candle to burn completely, the ashes can be sprinkled to the wind.

In any spell I work, especially one that involves money I like to say 'and harm to none' at some point during the working, and don't be too greedy, only ask for what you really need.

Autumn Equinox meditation:

Make yourself comfortable, close your eyes and focus on your breathing, deep breaths in...deep breaths out...

As your world around you dissipates you find yourself standing on a footpath in the middle of a large forest, there is a chill in the air but the sun is shining. All around you are beautiful trees dressed in their autumn foliage, so many wonderful colours – oranges, reds, yellows, browns and greens, it is breathtaking.

You start to walk along the pathway, which is strewn with fallen leaves of every colour. You can feel the change in the air, the autumn chill. There are trees here of every species.

As you walk you look around you, taking in the colours and the size and shape of all the trees, you also look on the ground and see fallen nuts and seeds, something in the undergrowth catches your eye and you bend down to pick it up. It is a gift from Mother Nature for you, take it with you and ponder on its message to you later.

Suddenly something darts across the pathway and shoots up the trunk of a tree. You stop and stand very still looking to see what it was. As you look into the boughs of the tree you see a squirrel, its cheeks stuffed full to bursting with something that it has taken to hide away for the winter. You watch as it stashes away its hoard, it looks like acorns.

You stand a while and watch the squirrel work, thinking about your own abundance and blessings and what you will look forward to over the winter months. Think about the things that you have finished with and can move on from, then about the projects and new directions you can take over winter, when the days are shorter and the evenings are dark...

You see the squirrel dart back down the tree and scoot across the pathway again and he has gone… disappeared into the trees, no doubt to collect more acorns.

You carry on walking down the pathway for a while, stopping every so often to connect with a tree, putting your hands out to touch the bark and feeling the energy of each tree, each one individual, each one different. Thanking the tree as you leave it.

When you are ready, take one last look around at the autumn beauty the woodland has to offer and then slowly and gently come back to this reality.

Wriggling your fingers and toes and stretching your arms and legs, open your eyes.

Samhain

31st October/1st November

(pronounced sow-een or sow-ain)

Samhain is generally celebrated on 31st October, when most people celebrate Halloween. Although it is also celebrated on 1st November as well. It is the end of summer and marks the last harvest. It is also a time when the veil between the worlds is at its thinnest, a time when we can connect with spirit.

We celebrate Samhain to mark the last harvest, but also to honour our ancestors and those who have gone before us. At this point in the year our ancestors would have taken their excess cattle and livestock to be slaughtered and then preserved to last them over the coming dark winter months.

For witches Samhain also marks the end of the old year and the beginning of the new. It is a time to reflect on what we have achieved over the preceding months and a time to make resolutions and plans for the following ones.

I always celebrate this Sabbat with added enthusiasm as 31st October also marks my birthday. Even as a child I was given gifts of witches, dragons and faeries because of the date my birth fell upon, guess it was a sign LOL! I always decorate our front bay window with a mixture of a traditional witch's tools but also with some fun Halloween decorations as well. We always have lots of trick or treaters too so the evening is usually great fun adding in some form of divination and also honouring of the dead as well.

Symbols

I am sure you will know the symbols for Samhain already but here are the ones I associated with this Sabbat: pumpkins, gourds, black pointy hats, broomsticks, black cats, bats, skeletons, skulls, spiders, wolves and Moons.

In the garden

Not a lot going on in the garden at this time of the year. If you have been lucky enough not to get a frost yet, some of the late flowers might be struggling through still, but generally it is a time to finish tidying up and getting everything ready for the winter slumber.

Herbs

Mugwort, allspice, mandrake, sage, rosemary, chrysanthemum and deadly nightshade.

Foods

Pumpkin (of course!), apples, root vegetables, mulled wines, meat, candy, ale, cider and mushrooms.

Colours

Black, orange, white, silver, gold and red

Activities:

All forms of divination.

Make a witches ladder adding your intent for new projects for the coming months.

Make resolutions. Write them on small slips of paper and then burn them in a candle flame.

Ancestors altar

Make an ancestors altar. This can be as simple as a photograph of a grandparent who has passed over. Find a suitable space, a shelf or a small table, but don't put your ancestor altar in the bedroom. Use a black or white cloth as the base and put out photographs of your ancestors, you could also add a crystal ball if you have one. You can also add mementos if you have them, old pieces of jewellery and ornaments you have inherited. Add white candles. Leave offerings of food or drink and make sure to change them regularly.

A dumb supper

This is a lovely way to honour the dead. I am not sure how old the tradition is, but it is fun to work with.

The first thing to do is decide which room you are going to hold your dumb supper in and make it a sacred space by casting a circle or smudging the area. Make sure there are not electrical items turned on in the room such as televisions or telephones.

The main theme of a dumb supper is silence. It is not a miserable, solemn silence, but one of respect.

When you invite your guests ask each one to bring along a note to the dinner, which should contain what they wish to say to any friends or relatives that have passed over. Don't ask what is in the note, this is private for them.

Set a place at your dining table for each guest, but keep the head of the table empty, this is for the spirits. Place a small candle, tea lights work well, at the place setting for spirit, one candle for each deceased person you wish to honour. The chair at this place setting can also be covered with a white or black cloth.

No one is permitted to speak as they enter the dining room and not at any time during the entire supper. As each guest enters the room they take a moment and stop at the spirit chair. This is when they can take a moment to honour the dead.

Once each person has taken their place at the table, everyone joins hands and all offer a silent blessing to the deceased.

No one should start eating until everyone has been served and that includes a serving for spirit.

When the meal is finished, each guest may then bring out their personal notes to the dead. In turn each person goes to the place setting of spirit. They focus on the message they have written, then they catch the edge of the note in the flame of one of the candles and burn it – it is also a good idea to have a small cauldron or fire proof dish at this place setting too! When everyone has taken their turn they all join hands once again in a further blessing.

Once this is all done everyone may leave the room, still in silence, stopping at the chair of spirit to give a final blessing.

Incense

Mint, nutmeg, patchouli, myrrh, copal, clove, marigold, sage, mugwort, sandalwood and heliotrope.

Samhain incense recipe

Sage
Myrrh
Mugwort
Marigold
Sandalwood
Patchouli

Blend them all together.

Oils

Basil, camphor, clove, frankincense, yarrow, ylang ylang, patchouli, rosemary, ginger, cinnamon and myrrh

Samhain oil recipe

Blend together the following essential oils, with a base oil:

Clove
Frankincense
Patchouli
Rosemary

Samhain oil recipe 2

Blend together the following essential oils, with a base oil:

Myrrh
Cinnamon
Ginger

Spell workings

Samhain is a good time for workings involving divination, psychic abilities, new beginnings, banishing, past lives, astral projection, clearing, inner work and manifesting.

Seed charm for the ancestors

This charm is for honouring those who have passed over, it can be for humans or animals. The seeds are grown in memory of your loved ones. You will need:

A packet of seeds, doesn't matter what type but try to pick something that can be easily grown
A dish
A white candle in a holder
A bag to hold the seeds

The night before Samhain put the seeds into the dish and light the candle beside it. Visualise the person, people or animals that you wish to remember and honour. You could even say a few words if you like in their memory. Leave the seeds overnight in the dish and let the candle burn out completely (keep an eye on it so that you don't burn the house down...)

On Samhain take the seeds from the dish and put them in the bag. Take the bag in your power hand and, standing over the pot or area of earth you wish to plant them in, think again about that person or animal and remember them, then scatter the seeds over the earth.

The seeds will obviously take some time to germinate and it won't happen until spring, but then it will be a reminder to you that you honour your ancestors and those who have gone before you.

Crafts

Tin lanterns

Materials required:

Treacle tin or similar (clean and empty)
Picture hanging wire
Bradawl

Empty and clean the tin. Clean the tin inside and out with hot water and then make sure it is dry. Use the bradawl to carefully push holes through the tin to make a pattern. If you are going for a particular design then you might want to mark it out with marker pen first – take care not to slip and hurt yourself as the metal on the tin is slippery and edges can be sharp.

Punch two holes at the top of the tin on opposite sides ready for the hanging wire. Loop the wire through and twist each end close to the tin to form the handle. Turn the lid upside down and push through into the tin to provide and extra base. Add a tealight.

NOTE: the tin will get HOT!

Vision board

I like to make a vision board at Samhain, one that sets me up for projects and goals to take me through the winter months.

All you need is a pin board, a piece of cardboard you can stick pictures to or you can make a collage on the computer.

A vision board is a visualisation tool to help you achieve your goals, dreams and wishes.

Cut out pictures from old magazines, draw pictures or print images from the internet to create your own board.

The images that you need are ones that really speak to you. If you want more happiness in your life use a picture of someone smiling or jumping for joy. If you want to bring more love into your life pin a picture of a red or pink heart to your board. If you want to move to a particular town or country pin an image of that place onto your board.

All the images you use will be personal to you and will work with your subconscious to create the state of mind you want and to help focus you in the direction you need to go to meet those goals.

Your board needs to inspire you, so keep changing and adding to it on a regular basis and remember to hang it somewhere prominent so that you will see it every day.

Pumpkins

Now I am not going to tell you how to carve pumpkins because I am sure you all know how to do that! But how about painting onto pumpkins instead of carving them? There are lots of Halloween themed stencils on the internet, print one off and use spray paint or dab acrylic paint with a sponge over the stencil to create the images on your pumpkin – good results and no squishy pumpkin mess. You don't have to just use pumpkins, try squashes, gourds or turnips. Go smaller still and paint acorns or hazelnuts to look like tiny pumpkins!

Black mirror

A wonderful way to scry is to use a black mirror and they are really easy to make. Find an old photo frame or picture frame that has a glass front. Take the glass out and paint one side of it with black paint. Cut a piece of black velvet or soft black cloth to the same size as the glass and put that behind it. Put the glass back into the frame and voila! You have a ready to go scrying mirror.

The best time to use your mirror is at dusk or night time, if you can sit with the mirror in front of you and manage to get the moonlight shining in on the mirror even better. If not, just set a lit candle near the mirror so that it casts some reflections.

Relax and think about a question or a situation and then look into the mirror. You might see images, you might see shapes, just relax and see what comes to you.

When you have finished looking in the mirror make sure to jot down what you saw so that you can look back over it and hopefully make some sense of it!

Pumpkin candle holders

If you can get hold of some small pumpkins, they make excellent tea light holders, you could also use large apples for this as well. Hollow out a space in the top of the pumpkin so that a tea light just sits nicely inside and that's it! Pumpkin candle holder made.

Waxed leaves

Pick up a nice selection of autumn leaves, then melt some candle wax. For this you can use up all the old candle stubs you have collected. When the wax is melted, carefully, and I mean carefully because hot candle wax is horrible on your skin (speaking from personal experience), dip each leaf into the wax, coating both sides, then lay the leaves on greaseproof paper to dry. Once they are set you can use them for all sorts of decoration ideas.

Halloween tree

Using a tall vase, fill it with a mixture of rice and wild rice then stick twigs into it to make a 'tree'. You can then hang Hallowe'en decorations and candy from the twigs.

Day of the Dead skulls

El Dia de los Muertos – the Day of the Dead – and the tossing of Mexican culture into the melting pot of America. This celebration begins on the eve of October 31st. It is often called Los Dias de los Muertos because more than one day is involved, depending on the local celebration. My most favourite symbols from the Day of the Dead are the skulls. Using a basic skull shape, they are decorated in wild and beautiful colours and made from sugar, chocolate, bread and candy. You can buy Day of the Dead skull moulds in a lot of craft shops and they come with instructions, but I like to make a simpler version using felt.

I draw out a basic skull shape and use it as a template to cut two pieces of felt. I then decorate one piece with buttons, embroidery stitches, sequins and jewels in a Day of the Dead pattern. I then sew the other piece of felt to the back and stuff it with dried beans and herbs as I do when I make a poppet.

Samhain wreath

Using a basic wreath shape available in craft stores – foam or wicker – you can add all sorts of Halloween items to it, such as autumn leaves, dried apple slices, tiny plastic bats and spiders. Make little tiny tombstones from cardboard, use lots of yellow and black ribbon and tiny pumpkins. You could even cover the wreath shape with dried pumpkin seeds or Hallowe'en candy.

Samhain meditation

Make yourself comfortable and close your eyes, focus on your breathing, deep breathes in…deep breathes out…

As your world around you dissipates you find yourself at the bottom of a mountain. The grass is green and lush beneath your feet and the air is clear and crisp.

You hear the trickling sound of water and look to your left to see a stream, crystal clear water bubbles its way between large craggy rocks and over small grey stones. Perched on one of the large grey rocks is a big black raven. He turns and stares at you with his beady, all knowing eye… he squawks, flaps his wings and flies off in the direction of the mountain.

As you turn and watch him go you see a small pathway that meanders up the side of the mountain, so you decide to follow it.

The path is narrow but easy going. As you walk you take in the beautiful scenery; autumnal fields scattered with grey rocks, as if someone had stood on top of the mountain and thrown a handful of them, the rocks lying in the grass where they fell.

As you come around a bend in the path you see an old woman sitting bent over a cauldron, which hangs over a fire. She is dressed in black with a shawl drawn tightly around her shoulders, she is muttering to herself and dropping what looks like herbs into the bubbling liquid in the cauldron.

As you approach her you catch the scent of the stew on the air, it smells delicious.

She sees you and without a word beckons you to join her.

You seat yourself on the ground next to her as she slowly lowers herself onto a small three-legged stool.

You sit in silence for a while until she brings out an old earthenware cup and ladles a spoonful of the stew into it and offers it to you.

You accept it and take a sip, it tastes as wonderful as it smells. As you do this, the old woman speaks for the first time in a voice that sounds as ancient as the mountains themselves. She tells you that with each sip from the cup you must release something that no longer serves you, a bad memory, a negative emotion or perhaps a habit you wish to be rid of.

As you sip the stew you pay heed to her words and do as she asks.

Once you have finished all the stew in the cup the old woman takes it from you and presses something into your now empty hand. She tells you that it is a gift to represent positive energy to replace the void that the released memories and emotions have made.

She tells you to leave and as you do, with each step you must believe that you are heading into new beginnings, taking a fresh look at your life and living to the fullest, making new plans and moving forward with a happy heart and soul.

You turn to thank the old woman, but she has already gone. Sitting in the place that she had occupied is the raven. He fixes you with his stare, squawks again and flies off back down the pathway.

You follow his direction and return down the pathway, putting into action the old woman's instructions.

When you reach the bottom of the mountain you feel a sense of rebirth, full of inspiration and positive energy.

Slowly bring yourself back to this reality.

Wriggling your fingers and toes and stretching your arms and legs, open your eyes.

Winter Solstice

20th - 22nd December

Yule

This is one of my favourite times of the year. I do celebrate Christmas with my family as I am the only pagan, but none of my family are particularly religious themselves. They have always treated it as a time of year to get together, to eat (and drink) and spend time as a family.

Christmas as a child was always spent surrounded by my parents, my brother, grandparents, uncle, aunt and four cousins along with various pets. It was total chaos but we loved it.

I love the build up to the festive season, I especially like putting up decorations – I have two huge Yule trees and each one I decorate with baubles (witches' balls), cinnamon sticks tied with ribbon, pentacles made out of twigs, red berry decorations and lots of twinkling lights. My altars I decorate in reds and greens using lots of ivy, holly and mistletoe.

Yule is the Winter Solstice. It marks the shortest day and the longest night of the year. It is the time of the year when the Holly King and the Oak King battle again, this time the Oak King is victorious and lives to reign over the lighter half of the year to come.

Symbols

Holly, ivy, mistletoe, candles, Yule logs, poinsettia, wreaths and bells.

In the garden

There is not a lot going on outside at this time of the year. I just remember to leave food out for the birds regularly as there isn't much about in nature to keep them sustained. Also leave out fresh water if it is icy.

Herbs

Oak, sage, bay, pine, frankincense, ginger, orange, holly, ivy, juniper, mistletoe, myrrh, cinnamon and pine cones.

Foods

Turkey (of course), nuts, roasted meats, oranges, dried fruits, mincemeat, egg nog, gingerbread, chocolate and mulled wine.

Colours

Red, dark green, gold, silver and white.

Activities

Spend time with family and friends, reminiscing over old times and making new memories.

Light candles to celebrate the return of the sun.

Light a bonfire outside and have an outdoor BBQ or party (wrap up warm!).

Go wassailing. Wassail is a hot spicy drink usually made with apple juice or cider. People process to the local orchard and pour wassail under an apple tree to bring a good harvest.

Go for a walk in the woods and collect pine cones to decorate with glitter and hang on the Yule tree and collect a log to make into a Yule log. When collecting pine cones, it is important to leave behind the cones that haven't opened. The seeds from these cones should be left so that animals such as squirrels have something to eat. Find cones that have the tips spread open.

Incense

Bayberry, pine, cinnamon, clove, all spice, frankincense, myrrh, nutmeg and orange.

Yule incense recipe

Pine
Frankincense
Cinnamon
Dried orange peel

Blend them all together.

Oils

Cedar, ginger, cinnamon, pine, frankincense, myrrh, juniper and nutmeg.

Yule oil recipe 1

Blend together the following essential oils, with a base oil:

Juniper

Pine
Frankincense
Cedar

Yule oil recipe 2

Blend together the following essential oils, with a base oil:

Cinnamon
Clove
Orange

Spell workings

Honouring yourself, family and friends. Inner work, personal rebirth.

Yule spell

Make your Yule decorations magical.

Tie cinnamon sticks together with red ribbon for love and passion. Or tie them together with green ribbon for prosperity and success.

Pine cones are plentiful at this time of year. Burn one in your cauldron to banish negative energy and purify ritual space. Put a pine cone in the corner of each room in your home for protection.

Dust pine cones with glitter and place a whole heap of them in a glass vase, not only do they look pretty but they will also work magically for prosperity and protection.

Pine cones can also be carried with you for fertility.

Crafts

Miniature Yule log ornaments

These are good for decorating your Yulc trcc, but are also nice for table presents for guests.

You will need:

A stick about an inch thick
Red wool or ribbon
Small feathers
Small pieces of evergreen plants – pine, fir, spruce, or similar
Seed beads in your choice of colours
A hot glue gun

Cut the stick into 2in to 3in lengths. Decorate each small log with the feathers, evergreens and seed beads in a design you like. Tie a piece of red wool or ribbon around the centre and knot in a bow.

Use the ribbon to tie it to your tree or you could add a small piece of card with your guest's name on for a table place setting.

Pine cone decorations

You will need:

Pine cones (obviously!)
Equal amounts of cinnamon, nutmeg and allspice, mixed together
A 1:1 mixture of water and craft glue
Glitter
Ribbon
A small paintbrush

Run the pine cones under water for a few seconds then spread them out on a baking sheet. Bake in the oven at 250 degrees for about 20 minutes. The baking process makes the pine cones open up and also destroys any bacteria that might be lurking on them. If you obtained your pine cones from a craft shop you will be able to skip this step.

Cool the pine cones and then apply the glue mix. It is up to you whether you coat the entire pine cone with glue or just the odd petal or just the tips – be creative!

Mix together the spices and the glitter, then shake the mix onto the pine cones or alternatively (and probably the least messy option) iput the spice/glitter mix into a plastic bag then drop the pine cones in and give them a shake.

Once the glue on the pine cone is dry you can tie a piece of ribbon around it and use it to hang on your Yule tree.

Reindeer food

We made this last year and it was great fun. We sprinkled the reindeer food on the pathway by the front door so that the Holly King (Santa) knew where to land.

What you need:

Oatmeal
Coloured sugar crystals
Dried cranberries

Mix together the ingredients (start with enough oatmeal for your needs then add the sugar and cranberries in spoonfuls until you get the right mixture).

You can put the mixture in a jar or bag and tie with a ribbon to give as a gift, then the night before Yule sprinkle on the pathway (it is all biodegradable).

Bay balls

What you need:

Foam ball shape (from craft shops)
Bay leaves – preferably fresh, if you use dry ones soak them overnight
Glue

Starting at the bottom of the foam ball, stick the bay leaves around it, slightly overlapping each one. Work your way up the ball until you reach the top. You can also add cloves to help hold some of the leaves in place if they stubbornly refuse to lie flat (some of them do).

Pin a loop of ribbon or cord to the top to hang it up with.

Golden acorns

What you need:

Acorns – obviously!
Spray or craft paint
Ribbon

Separate the acorn from its little cap and paint both pieces. Leave to dry, then using a slim piece of ribbon about 3ins long, glue each end of the ribbon inside the acorn cap so that it makes a loop. Then glue the cap back onto the acorn. You can also add a bit of glitter if you would like to.

Salt dough decorations

Salt dough is one of the easiest things in the world to make, and you can create just about anything from it. Use it with cookie cutters to make your own Sabbat ornaments.

What you need:

4 cups (33oz) flour
1 cup (8oz) salt
1 ½ cups (12 fl oz) hot water
1 tsp vegetable oil

Combine the salt and flour, then add the water until the dough becomes elastic. Add the oil at this time and knead the dough (if it's too sticky, add more flour). Once it's a good consistency, make your decorations with cookie cutters. Bake ornaments at 200 degrees until hard (about 20-30 minutes). Once they've cooled, paint them with designs and symbols, and seal with clear varnish. If you're planning to hang them, poke a hole through the ornament BEFORE baking them. Then, after you've varnished them, run a ribbon or thread through the hole. You can also add a teaspoon of cinnamon and/or some glitter into the mixture too!

Pine cone wreath

Pine cones are excellent for making wreaths. After you bring home the cones and allow them to dry, you need a wreath base to attach the cones to. A pizza box or other sturdy cardboard could be used to make a doughnut shape or any other shape you might like. You can attach the cones with a hot glue gun or tub and tile caulk that comes in tubes. You can add other natural materials such as dried flowers, leaves, moss, or stones if you like. Attach a wire loop to the back of the wreath and hang.

Dress up your candles for Yule

You can do this with existing candles... it's quick and easy.

Tie on coloured ribbons or raffia, glue on tiny pine cones to make a pattern. Use brass tacks or silver pins to make patterns by pushing them into the candle. Stick on shells, cinnamon pieces and even coffee beans to decorate it.

I like to sprinkle herbs and spices onto the top of a candle I have dressed with essential oil and then drip contrasting wax from another candle on top to seal the herbs and spices in and to make it pretty.

Yule wish tree

Using a small evergreen Yule tree in a pot, during the days leading up to Yule get each member of your family and group of friends to tie a coloured ribbon (red, green and white ribbons work well) onto the tree to represent a wish or a blessing.

Once Yule is over keep the tree well watered and looked after. Then, on the 1st February, take off all the ribbons and burn them, casting the ashes to the wind.

Yule meditation

Make yourself comfortable and close your eyes, focus on your breathing, deep breathes in…deep breathes out…

As your world dissipates you find the air around you becoming very cold, but you are warmly dressed. The ground beneath your feet is covered in crisp, white snow that crunches under foot. As you breathe your breath comes out in clouds of mist, like dragon breath.

As you look up you see the dark imposing image of a stone circle on the skyline, the stone circle of Stonehenge.

The sun is rising behind the stone circle, the sky is a beautiful kaleidoscope of colours.

You make your way across the white blanket of snow towards the stones, you feel the cold air on your face and feel the snow beneath your feet.

Once you reach the stones you put out your hand to touch the surface of one of the outer standing stones, it feels warm and you can feel an old and ancient energy pulsing through it.

You step between two of the outer stones and enter the inner circle. You can feel the energy spiralling between the stones.

You move to stand in the centre of the circle and turn to watch as the sun rises, its rays breaking through the stones and bathing you in the golden light of the Winter Solstice sun. You soak up the sunlight and feel the energy from the rays, filtering through the stones.

As you are watching the horizon, you see movement out of the corner of your eye. You turn to see a fox creeping about by one of the large outer stones. It stops still and looks up as it realises you are watching, your eyes lock for a split second then it dashes across the centre circle and disappears. All that is left are the footprints it has left in the snow.

Feeling refreshed, renewed and full of energy, you turn and walk back out of the stone circle through the inner stones and to the outer stones. As you exit you turn and place your hand on one of the large standing stones, feeling once more the special energy it contains.

Then slowly you make your way out and back across the field to where you started. Gently bringing yourself back to this reality.

Wriggling your fingers and toes and stretching your arms and legs, open your eyes.

Imbolc

1st/2nd February
(Pronounced im-bulk)

The beginnings of spring. When the earth begins to stir and life begins to awaken. It is the time of year when livestock will start to give birth to the first young of the year. It can also be the coldest time in the dark half of the year. The farmers start to plough their fields now in preparation for planting.

This festival is also known sometimes as Candlemas.

It is a time for purification, for renewal and new beginnings. This festival is one dedicated to the Maiden aspect of the Goddess and it is usually attributed to the Goddess Brighid (also called Bride or Brigit).

Symbols

Besoms, candle wheels, Brighid's cross, acorn-tipped wands (priapic wands), ploughs, lambs, white flowers, wells and candles.

In the garden

This depends on the weather, which to be honest in the UK has been totally unpredictable recently! You may start to see crocus and snowdrops appearing.

Herbs

Bay, iris, violets, rosemary, dill, basil, pine, cinnamon, rose, frankincense, myrrh and angelica.

Foods

All varieties of seeds, scones, all dairy products – milk, cheese, butter, onions, garlic, herbal teas.

Colours

White, yellow, pale green and pale pink.

Activities

Light lots of white candles to bring purification and renewal into your home.

Go for walks in your area to see if you can spot the first signs of spring.

Meet with friends and ask them all to bring a candle. Sit together and light the candles, reflecting on that which you wish to release and move on from and focus on what you wish to bring into your life.

Have a good 'spring clean' in your house, sweep through with a besom to clear away any stale or negative energies.

Cleanse and reconsecrate all your magical tools.

Incense

Bay, violet, myrrh, basil, chamomile, frankincense, dragon's blood, cinnamon, sandalwood, dill seeds, orange peel, bergamot and rose petals.

Imbolc incense recipe

Frankincense
Dragon's blood
Sandalwood
Bergamot

Cinnamon

Blend them all together.

Oils

Benzoin, pine, cedar, orange, basil, frankincense, myrrh, sandalwood, jasmine

Imbolc oil recipe 1

Blend together the following essential oils, with a base oil:

Chamomile
Rosemary
Basil

Imbolc oil recipe 2

Blend together the following essential oils, with a base oil:

Cedar
Frankincense
Pine
Orange
Rose

Spell workings

Growth, renewal, re-birth, fertility, purification. Releasing the old to make way for the new.

New self potato spell

If there is an aspect of your personality that you would like to let go of, then this spell is perfect.

What you need:

A potato

A knife
A slip of paper and a pen

Write what it is you want to let go of, the aspect that you wish to release, onto the slip of paper.

Cut a slit into the potato large enough for you to be able to place the slip of paper into (you can fold it up).

Visualise that aspect being released and put the slip of paper into the potato.

Then take the potato and bury it into your garden. This takes the aspect you want to be released from and consigns it to Mother Earth.

Crafts

Candle wheel

Materials needed:

Foam wreath
Eight white candles
Ivy leaves, vines or seasonal flowers and foliage
Glue gun

Dig out eight holes at equal spacings around the wreath so that you can sit the candles in it, or fix small candle holders onto the wreath using a glue gun.

Decorate around the candles with ivy leaves or your seasonal flowers and foliage.

The eight candles represent the eight Sabbats in the Wheel of the Year, the circle of the wreath is particularly important at Imbolc.

Brighid's bed

Materials needed:

Basket, box, doll cradle or similar item (I have even made a tiny one using a match box)
Small blanket cut offs or material to use as bedding
Figure to represent the goddess Brighid

Dress up the box, cover it with wrapping paper or paint it in a design of your choice.

You can make a figure to represent Brighid, it could be made out of Fimo clay, straw or even a tiny dolly. Keep it simple and if you dress it make sure it is wearing white to represent the Maiden.

Lay the figure in the bed on top of the covers.

Place your Brighid's bed in an inviting part of your home, it is to show that she is welcome in your house. Ask for her blessings of fertility and healing.

Ice candles

This craft combines the symbolic candle with snowflakes, as February usually still has snow (depending on where you live of course).

What you need:

Ice
Paraffin wax or old candle stubs
A taper candle
A cardboard container such as a juice or milk carton
A double boiler, or two pans

Firstly melt the wax in the double boiler. Always use a double boiler/two pans because the wax can catch fire if it comes in direct contact with heat.

While the wax melts, prepare your candle mould – place the taper candle in the middle of the cardboard carton, then fill the carton with ice, packing it loosely around the taper candle. (It works best if you use small ice cubes).

Once the wax has melted pour it into the container very carefully, making sure it fills the carton evenly around the ice. As the wax goes in it will melt the ice and leave small holes in the candle.

When the candle is cool make a small hole in the bottom of the carton so that the melted water can drain out (put it in a bowl or hold it over the sink). Leave the candle in the carton overnight so that it hardens fully.

Then you can peel off the cardboard carton and you will have a beautiful ice candle.

Imbolc meditation

Make yourself comfortable and focus on your breathing, deep breaths in…deep breaths out…

As your world dissipates you find yourself in a clearing, it is dusk and the Moon is showing her beautiful face to light your way.

All around the edge of the clearing are candles, lots and lots of candles, their flames flickering slightly in the breeze.

You can hear faint sounds around you. They are the sound of animals, of sheep and their newborn lambs stirring as the darkness falls.

In the candlelight and the light of the Moon you can make out something in the centre of the clearing. As you walk towards it you realise it is flowers, tiny white flowers, they are snowdrops, the first ones of the season having pushed their way up through the earth, making their new beginnings.

You sit yourself down next to the flowers and make yourself comfortable. You focus on the candles with their flames flickering. Watch them as the light breeze makes the flames dance to its tune.

With the sound of the newborn lambs in your ears and with the light of the dancing candle flames in your eyes, focus on what you need to let go of in your life, what thoughts, emotions and events you need to release. Let the light of the Moon and the candle flames cleanse you of any unwanted emotions and thoughts.

Then focus on what you want to fill your life with, new ideas, new projects, and new beginnings. Focus on moving forward, starting afresh with a new outlook on life.

Be positive, be strong, be focused, be honest and truthful to your own inner voice, listen to your intuition, be YOU.

When you are ready, stand and walk towards the edge of the clearing and slowly walk around the boundary, careful snuffing out each candle. As you do so let that candle take away each negative thought.

Once you are done, slowly and gently bring yourself back to this reality.

Wriggle your fingers and toes and stretch your arms and legs. Open your eyes.

Spring Equinox

20th - 22nd March

Ostara

The festival of chocolate ;-) Well that's what it seems like and I can live with that…

Ostara is a celebration of the Spring Equinox, the signs of spring should be well under way and new planting of crops and flowers should be happening. It is a time when day and night are equal. All of nature is stirring and showing signs of activity after its winter slumber. The power of the sun will increase and the days will start to become longer than the nights.

This is the festival of fertility and sowing of seeds. Spring is sprung!

Symbols

Hares, chicks, eggs, rabbits, spring flowers, lambs, baskets and the Green Man.

In the garden

New life should be springing up in the garden now, new shoots should be beginning on the trees and plants, spring flowers should be starting to bloom. Just keep an eye out for frosts still.

Herbs

Broom, ginger, jasmine, mugwort, sage, St John's wort, vervain.

Foods

Eggs, fish, honey, lamb, dandelions, nettles, dairy foods, hot cross buns, green vegetables, sweets, edible flowers and chocolate (did I mention chocolate already).

Colours

Pastel colours – blue, yellow, pink, green and white.

Activities

Take a walk in your local area and smile and celebrate the signs of spring, not just the plants but the wild animals, birds and insects too.

Paint eggs and hide them for an egg hunt.

Go to a local park or beach and pick up litter, help the Earth by cleansing it of rubbish.

Perform egg divination (called oomancy). Separate the whites from the yolks, then drop the white into a bowl of hot water and see what symbols or shapes it makes.

Light black and white candles around your home to symbolise the dark and the light – this reminds us of the balance in life and within ourselves.

Incense

Ginger, jasmine, mugwort, sage, nutmeg, vervain, rose, magnolia, violet, orange peel and willow.

Spring Equinox incense recipe

Frankincense
Nutmeg
Violet
Orange
Rose

Blend the ingredients together.

Oils

Hyacinth, lily, rose, violet, strawberry, lotus, myrrh, elder, ginger, geranium, patchouli, chamomile, cedarwood and broom.

Spring Equinox oil recipe 1

Blend together the following essential oils, with a base oil:

Rose
Geranium
Chamomile
Myrrh
Cedarwood

Spring Equinox oil recipe 2

Blend together the following essential oils, with a base oil:

Lavender
Violet
Elder
Patchouli

Spell workings

Renewal and rebirth, new beginnings and balance, inspiration, changes, new opportunities and hope.

Egg spell

This spell is so simple and is good for bringing something back into your life such as money, luck, friendship or love, in fact the possibilities are endless. Don't aim this spell at any one person, just aim at bringing about circumstances to achieve your desired goal.

What you need:

An egg
Boiling water in a bowl or pan

Place the egg into the boiling water, the watch the egg, visualise that which you would like to manifest into your life, imagine that desire is inside the egg shell, waiting to be released.

Watch the egg for about five minutes, visualising as you do so.

Then remove the egg from the water and allow it to cool. You can decorate the shell if you wish with designs or symbols that represent your goal.

Bury the egg either in your garden by your door or in a plant pot outside your doorway. Each time you walk past it re-affirm your goal. The egg will start to break down and decompose within the soil, as it does so it will release your desire.

Crafts

Ostara seed cards

These are a lovely idea for greetings cards. You could adapt them and use them for birthday cards too.

You will need:

Card or pre-cut card templates
Envelopes
Seed packets

Glue (PVA is suitable. Do not use a glue gun as the heat can damage the seeds.)
Pens

If using a plain sheet of card, fold it over to make a card shape. Using the glue, stick a seed packet to the front of the card.

Using pens of your choice write your message inside the card.

Ostara tree

You will need:

Several large twigs (use windfalls collected from the ground around the tree)
Florist's foam
A flower pot
Paint
Decorations

Paint the flower pot with spring designs. Be creative, adding butterflies, eggs or flowers or just paint it a spring colour.

Fit a piece of florist's foam into the flowerpot and then stick the twigs into the foam so that it forms the shape of a tree.

Then decorate! Hang painted eggs or chocolate treats onto the branches.

Home-dyed eggs

Simple but very effective! These can be used for an egg hunt.

What you need:

Eggs
A pan of water
Vinegar
Natural ingredients for making the colours

Start with your pan of boiling water with a teaspoon of vinegar added, make sure there is enough water in the pan to cover the eggs and it works best if you only boil three or four at a time.

Then carefully add your eggs to the water.

To colour the eggs add one of the items listed below. Try different amounts to get different shades, but it will take about 20 minutes of simmering to get the colour to set into the shells.

Red/pink: paprika, pomegranate or cranberry juice, beets or red onion skins
Purple: grape juice
Orange: onion skins
Yellow: lemon or orange peel, carrots or cumin
Gold: curry powder or turmeric
Brown: coffee or black walnut shells
Green: spinach
Blue: blueberries or red cabbage
Yellow/green: apple peel

Once they have achieved the colour you want, carefully remove them from the pan and place them on a paper towel to dry.

Keep the eggs in the fridge until you want to use them for your egg hunt. You can also paint the eggshells with a little glue and sprinkle with glitter too.

Drawing a design on the eggshell before you dye it with a wax crayon also creates a good effect.

Crystal eggs

These are wonderful and great fun for the children (and the adults).

What you need:

1 cup (8 oz) plain (all purpose flour)
½ cup (4oz) salt

½ cup (4 oz) sand
1 cup (8 oz) used coffee grounds
¾ cup (6 fl oz) warm water
Small crystals or gems
Non-stick cooking spray
Paint (acrylic works best)

Mix together the flour, salt, sand and coffee. Gradually add the water and knead until you have a thick dough (it will obviously feel a bit gritty).

Select a crystal and spray it with non-stick cooking oil and put it in the centre of a small ball of the dough. Shape the dough around the crystal and mould it into an egg shape.

Bake the eggs at 350 degrees for about 15 minutes and then allow them to cool.

Once they are cool they should feel and look like a rock. If you wish to, you can paint them in different colours.

The eggs can be used in an egg hunt or just given out for cracking open to reveal the hidden crystal.

Eggshell candles

What you need:

Uncooked eggs
Wax beads
Birthday candles
Knife

Make a small hole in the top (the pointed end) of the egg, chip away careful to make a small hole so that the raw egg inside can be tipped out. Chip away about a quarter of the eggshell.

Rinse the inside of the eggshell very carefully with warm water, and set it aside to dry.

Fill the shell half to three-quarters full with wax beads. Insert a birthday candle into the centre (you might need to trim the bottom of the birthday candle slightly to make it the right height).

Sit it in an egg cup or candle holder.

Eggshell plant pots

You will need:

Eggs
Egg carton
Fertiliser/soil
Cotton wool balls
Knife
Scissors
Plastic spoons
Seeds

Make a small hole in the top (pointed end) of the eggshell. Chip away about a quarter of the shell and allow the raw egg to pour out.

Wash the shell carefully in warm water and set to dry.

If you want to paint a design on your eggshell do so at this point, or draw a smiley face.

Put the eggshells in the egg carton with the hole at the top. Place a cotton wool ball into each eggshell. Spoon fertiliser into each egg shell. Sprinkle your seeds onto the soil, then sprinkle on a small amount of water, adding a trickle of water each day to keep the soil moist. Leave the egg planters in their carton on a sunny windowsill.

Once the seedlings are too big for the egg shells, crack the bottom of each shell so that the roots can grow through and plant in the garden or a plant pot, complete with the eggshell as this will break down and provide nutrients to the soil.

Ostara meditation

Make yourself comfortable, close your eyes and focus on your breathing, deep breaths in… and deep breaths out…

As the world around you dissipates you find yourself standing in a muddy track with fields either side of you. The sun is shining and the sky is a beautiful clear blue.

In the distance you can hear noises, a dog barking, chickens clucking and sheep bleating.

A dog comes suddenly dashing down the lane towards you. He was the source of the barking, as he reaches you he barks some more and turns and disappears back down the lane, so you follow him.

The earth is very wet and muddy underfoot, but you are dressed suitably and your boots make lovely squelching noises in the mud.

You follow the lane around and it opens out into the yard of a farm. It is surrounded on three sides by sheds and outbuildings, with a large tractor parked to one side.

As you reach the yard you see a bucket sitting in the middle of the pathway. You pick it up and realise that it is full of corn. As you lift the bucket hens and chicks come rushing out of one of the nearby barns. You take handfuls of the corn and scatter it on the ground, the chickens and baby chicks start to peck at it with great gusto.

Once the bucket is empty the hens start to head back to their barn, followed by all their tiny chicks, so you follow them too.

Inside the barn it is warm and smells of hay, the hens start to make themselves comfortable on bales of hay while the chicks snuggle up to their mothers. As you wander around you realise that all around the barn, nestled into the hay, are freshly laid eggs, and you still have the bucket with you, so you start looking and picking up all of the eggs and putting them into your basket. As you pick up each egg you think about the circle of life, of birth, living, death and rebirth and what it means to you. The egg is a complete symbol of this.

In among the eggs you spot something. You know it is a gift for you, a gift that has meaning. You pick it up and focus on it, what does it mean to you? What message does it carry? You think about it for a while then place it in your pocket.

Once you are finished you put the bucket of eggs by the barn door and make your way back out to the yard, retracing your footsteps across to the muddy lane and head back down to where your journey started from.

Slowly and gently come back to this reality.

Wriggling your fingers and toes and stretching your arms and legs, open your eyes.

Beltane

1st May

(Pronounced bell-tain)

Beltane heralds the coming of summer and is a festival of fertility. The seeds are sown, the plants and crops are all growing, the soil is fertile. This is the festival where we celebrate that fertility not just within the Earth, but within the union between the God and the Goddess and between humans too. It is the season to celebrate getting naked ;-) Celebrate love, happiness, union and life itself.

Our ancestors would have transferred their livestock from their winter shelter out to the fields and pastures and at this time the animals would have been driven between the Beltane bonfire to cleanse and purge them of evil spirits – as well as fleas – and to bring fertility.

Beltane is also a time when faeries are abound!

Symbols

Maypole, Beltane fires, May King and Queen, the Green Man, hobby horse, chalice, butterchurns, Jack in the Green, flower garlands, Pan.

In the garden

The plants in the garden should all be well under way now. Keep them protccted from any really late frosts. Give them all a good plant food to prepare them for the full on growing season.

Herbs

Ash, birch, bluebells, daisies, frankincense, ivy, lilac, primrose, rosemary, roses, cowslip, hawthorn, meadowsweet, clover and sorrel.

Foods

All dairy products, sweets, custards, ice cream, honey, oats, fruits, salads, barley and fruit punch.

Colours

Pastel colours, colours of the rainbow, red and white.

Activities

Get up early and watch the sun rise.

Spend an evening sitting around a camp fire with friends, then jump the fire leaving behind you anything that is hampering your life.

Beltane is also May Day, so make a Maypole and dance around it with friends!

Take a walk in your local woods and see if you can spot the first wild herbs of the season.

Take a picnic outdoors.

Wash your face in dew at sunrise on Beltane to keep your beauty in the coming year.

Find a local hawthorn tree and make a wish to the faeries. Take a strip of material or twine (please make sure it is biodegradable) and visualise your wish coming true, then tie the material to the tree sending your wish to the fae. Leave an offering for the tree too, some fertiliser or water.

Mark the boundaries of your property with oatmeal, this is a traditional Beltane grain and will provide protection.

Leave offerings of honey and milk in your garden or in the woods for the faeries.

Incense

Frankincense, lilac, rose, passion flower, angelica, copal, vanilla, cinnamon, honeysuckle, daffodil, dragon's blood

Beltane incense recipe

Dragon's blood
Hawthorn
Daffodil petals
Mugwort
Cinnamon

Blend the ingredients together.

Oils

Rose, lavender, jasmine, patchouli, ylang ylang, dragon's blood, coriander, myrrh, vervain, frankincense, neroli and sandalwood.

Beltane oil recipe 1

Blend together the following essential oils, with a base oil:

Rose
Dragon's blood
Coriander

Beltane oil recipe 2

Blend together the following essential oils, with a base oil:

Frankincense
Sandalwood

Rose
Jasmine

Spell workings

Making changes, spreading goodwill, setting goals, making plans, finding a focus and personal growth. Also prosperity, safety and love.

Beltane new project spell

Beltane is a wonderful time to begin a new project. With all the fertile and fire energy that this festival brings, you can channel that energy into your goal.

What you need:

Greenery/flowers
Green candle
Red candle
A natural item such as a shell, pebble or leaf
A small bag (cloth or paper)
If you have something green, it would be useful to wear it whilst working this spell.

Place fresh greenery and flowers on your altar (if you don't have an altar use a shelf or the table to create a sacred space for this working).

Light a red and a green candle.

Ground and centre yourself then pick up the shell, leaf or pebble and hold onto it for a few moments appreciating the wonder of Mother Nature and what she creates.

Place the item on the altar between the two candles and focus on it.

As you focus visualise your new project and how you want it to take shape. Be positive and creative!

Visualise all the energy and enthusiasm you have for your

project being focused on your item.

You might want to say an affirmation at this point.

Then when you are ready, extinguish the candles and place your item into a small bag. Keep the bag with you or on your altar, somewhere that you will see it regularly and be reminded of the energy and your goal.

Crafts

Maypole candle

You will need:

Small craft bells
Pastel coloured ribbons
White pillar candle

Cut the ribbon into lengths and tie a bell onto the end of each piece of ribbon. Tie the ribbons around the candle, just use knots not bows, you want the ribbons to trail.

If you have a tall candle stand that works very well to place the candle on, allowing the ribbons to trail down.

Braided headband

You will need:

9 ribbons, fairly narrow no more than ¼in wide and about 3ft to 6ft in length
Beads (with holes big enough to thread the ribbon through)

The colours of the ribbon are your choice, you might want to use the Triple Goddess colours of black, red and white, or the Triple God colours of black, green and yellow. You might want to stick to pastel colours for Beltane.

The length of ribbon will depend on how tall the person is

that the headband is for and how much ribbon you want to trail.

Lay the nine ribbons together with ends together, about a third of the way from one end tie them together in a knot. Thread a large bead on and push it up to the knot.

Separate the ribbons into sets of three and braid them. As you braid every couple of inches add a bead to one of the ribbons. Continue braiding until you have a third of the length left, then thread a large bead on and tie a knot to finish it off.

Green Man mask

You can either wear this at Beltane rituals or hang it above your altar as a symbol of this festival.

You will need:

Cardboard or craft foam to make the mask shape
Glue
Silk leaves
Piece of ribbon

Cut out a mask shape from the card or foam and punch a hole in either side to thread ribbon through to tie it around your head.

Lay out the design of your leaves first before you glue so that you get an idea of what pattern you want. It is easiest to start with the larger leaves around the outside and work your way in. Then start gluing the leaves on, overlapping each one slightly, but obviously leave holes for the eyes so you can see out!

Miniature Maypole

This makes a lovely ornament for your table or altar. The size depends on how big or small you want to make it.

You will need:

A branch or twig (of the size you require), but it needs to be fairly straight

Flowerpot
Cardboard
Pencil
Scissors
Glue
Sand
8 ribbons

If your stick has smaller twigs on it break them off so that it is fairly straight. It is up to you whether you keep the bark on or sand it smooth.

Then take your pot and draw around the bottom of it onto the cardboard. Insert the piece of cardboard into the bottom of the pot, this stops the sand from falling through the hole in the bottom.

Fill the flower pot halfway with sand then insert the stick into the middle, firm the sand down around it. Then fill the rest of the way up the pot with more sand, firming it down again so that the stick stand firm.

Tie the ribbons around the top of the stick, then fan them out or twist them around.

Beltane meditation

Make yourself comfortable, focus on your breathing, deep breaths in… deep breaths out…

As your world around you dissipates you find yourself on a village green. The sun is shining and you are surrounded by people laughing and talking.

You stand and watch for a moment, taking in everything around you. You are in the middle of a village fair, there are stalls all around with people serving cakes and drinks, a band with a fiddler are performing, and children are running around playing with hoops and skipping ropes.

You realise as you watch that this isn't modern day. The villagers are dressed simply and modestly, there are no cars, no mobile phones, and no signs of hectic life.

The houses surrounding the green are all beautifully brick built with perfect thatched roofs. The gardens to each one are full to bursting with spring flowers and the beginnings of early crops, the vegetables all mixed in with the flora.

Baskets of greenery hang from fences and gateways, brimming with spring flowers. The whole village is alive with life.

In the centre of the village green is a beautifully coloured Maypole. It is this that attracts your attention so you walk towards it.

A group of people are just about to start the Maypole dance. One of them indicates for you to join them, so you do. You are handed the end of a piece of coloured ribbon, what colour is it?

Then the music starts and the people in front of you and those behind you start to circle the Maypole. You catch the rhythm and start to dance along with them, weaving your ribbon in and out, over and under each one as you all dance together, the coloured ribbons slowly winding their way down and around the Maypole. Dance, enjoy, feel the energy of the music, the energy of life…

As the ribbons weave around and down you come to the bottom of the Maypole and the dancers start to slow down until they all stop, you stop with them.

You are elated, full of joy and anticipation.

The person you were dancing next to places a small flower into the palm of your hand. You thank them and look to see what it is…

When you look up again the villagers are starting to disperse, the music has stopped and people are packing away.

You make your way back across the green to the spot where you started.

Slowly and gently bring yourself back to this reality.

Wriggling your fingers and your toes, stretching your arms and legs, open your eyes.

Summer Solstice/Midsummer

20th - 23rd June
Litha

Litha is the Summer Solstice, it is midsummer – the longest day and the shortest night of the year.

The sun is at the height of its power, and although we hope that there are lots more days of summer to follow for a while, this is the point when the year starts to wane.

Solstice is a time to stand still, to stop and take stock of our lives and what we are doing, to celebrate what we have achieved and to acknowledge our failures, make sense of our actions and learn from them.

The Summer Solstice is a time to count our blessings, to celebrate life and pass on the spirit of generosity and goodwill.

The Earth is pregnant with the coming harvest and the Sun is at his peak.

The Summer Solstice sees the Oak King and the Holly King battle. This time the Holly King wins and reigns until the Winter Solstice.

Symbols

Fire, sun, oak trees, sun wheels, flowers, sunflowers, fruit, faeries, sickles, seashells and circles.

In the garden

The garden should be positively blooming at this point in the year, as well as hanging baskets and pots of summer flowers. The Summer Solstice is an excellent time to harvest herbs for drying to use in magical works. Herbs collected on the eve of midsummer, or early in the morning, have a special kind of energy. Remember to keep dead heading the flowers as this will encourage new ones, and I like to save the flower heads and dry them to use the petals in incense and magical workings.

Herbs

Chamomile, rose, honeysuckle, oak, lavender, ivy, yarrow, elder, thyme, carnation, mugwort, fennel, ginger, lemon, basil and St John's wort.

Foods

Fresh fruit and vegetables, honey, lemons, oranges, summer squash, ale, lemonade and mead.

Colours

Yellow, gold, green, blue, orange, white and red.

Activities

Get out in the sunshine! (But make sure you wear sun tan lotion and a hat).

Find a quiet spot outside to sit and meditate. Focus on the darkness and the light, not just within the world but within yourself too.

Go swimming at the beach or fill a paddling pool with water in your garden, failing that get the garden hose out ;-)

Have a bonfire in the warm summer evenings and a BBQ. Sit around the fire at dusk and tell stories or listen to music.

If you have a bonfire at the Summer Solstice, once the ashes of the fire have gone cold collect some to use as a protective amulet, pop them into a small pouch or mix with clay to make a talisman. You can also use some of the ashes to sprinkle on the garden to add nutrients to the soil.

This is also a good time to reaffirm your dedication to your path or your chosen tradition.

Incense

Lemon, myrrh, rose, wisteria, sandalwood, elder, fennel, ginger, frankincense, laurel, saffron, thyme and verbena.

Summer Solstice incense recipe

Mugwort
St John's wort
Frankincense
Sandalwood

Blend the ingredients together.

Oils

Chamomile, fennel, frankincense, ginger, rosemary, lavender, lemon, rose, heliotrope, mint and ylang ylang.

Summer Solstice oil recipe 1

Blend together the following essential oils, with a base oil:

Lavender
Rosemary
Mint

Summer Solstice oil recipe 2

Blend together the following essential oils, with a base oil:

Ylang ylang
Rose
Ginger
Rosemary

Spell workings

Abundance, wishes, love, healing and prosperity.

Litha wishes spell

This couldn't be easier. The Summer Solstice is a wonderful time to make wishes.

What you need:

A pebble, a feather or some herbs
A body of water such as the ocean, a stream or river
A slip of paper and a pen

Write down your wish on the slip of paper and then wrap that paper around a pebble, a feather or some herbs from your garden.

Visualise your wish, send your intent into the small parcel you have made and throw it into the running water.

Crafts

Sunshine ornaments

What you need:

Mug or cup
Scissors
Thin card
Gold paper
Pencil
Glue
Thin ribbon or thread
Needle

Use the mug or cup as a template to draw a circle on the cardboard. Then, using the cardboard template, trace and cut out 14 circles from the gold paper. Fold each circle in half, half and half again. When they are all done, unfold each one and cut along the fold lines, stopping about ½in from the centre.

Make the points of the sun by wrapping each of the eight segments around the point of a sharp pencil (facing away from the centre). Secure the points with glue.

Thread a needle with the thin ribbon or thread, you will need about an 18in length, and thread it through all the centres of the circles from the foil side of the first seven and the plain side of the remaining seven.

Very carefully pull the circles together to form a ball. Knot the ribbon or thread and leave the excess to make a hanging loop.

Hang them in your windows to reflect the sun.

Meditation beads

Your mind can sometimes tend to wander when you are meditating, which leads to a loss of concentration. For practising meditation, meditation beads can act as a kind of 'anchor' or grounding point enabling you to focus better. This can be extremely useful especially if you are feeling tired when you meditate.

Conversely, if your mind is too active and over-energised, meditation beads will prevent you from becoming distracted or daydreaming. And, because the beads are moved in rhythm with your breathing, it helps you maintain your concentration.

Meditation beads can be used in a number of ways. A popular method is to hang the string between your thumb and your third finger, traditionally in your right hand. Using your middle finger, you rotate the beads one bead at a time towards yourself, each time you repeat the mantra and take a breath.

A variation of this method is to hang the string on your middle finger and rotate the beads one at a time in the same fashion, only this time you use your thumb.

You begin the procedure at the first bead and repeat the process with all of the beads, continuing around the loop until you once again reach the start.

On my meditation beads, each bead signifies a different purpose – as I rotate the bead I say quietly to myself a mantra with that specific intent. For instance, when I reach the friends bead I say: 'I give thanks for my wonderful friends.' When I am on the Cailleach bead I say: 'I give blessings and honour the Cailleach for guiding me.'

On my meditation beads, each bead has a plain separator, then:

Green for abundance
Grey sparkly for the Cailleach
Wooden bead for the Green Man
Daisy for my friends
Brown for my family
World bead for the universe
Yellow for enlightenment
Pink for love
Black to release negativity
Light blue for healing
Orange for success
Clear for my totem Unicorn
Brown/red for my totem Wild Boar
Spiral for spirituality
Purple for wisdom
Spiral for balance
Red for empowering
Sparkly brown for happiness
Red for manifesting
Green for money
Blue for protection
Brown for strength
White for cleansing
Purple for meditation

You can have different beads for different purposes as I have done, or you can have a string of plain beads all the same colour. It is your choice, use whatever works for you.

Dream pillow

These dream pillows can be placed under your own pillow in your bed to bring you peaceful dreams.

What you need:

A piece of felt
Stuffing material
Dried lavender
Embroidery thread and a needle

I like to use an A4 size sheet of felt and fold it in half. Then I sew up two of the open sides with blanket stitch using embroidery thread. Then I fill it with some stuffing (I use odd leftover scraps of material or felt). Then I add a good handful of dried lavender flowers. I finish off by sewing up the open side.

Handfasting basket

The Summer Solstice is a popular time for people to get handfasted (the pagan 'marriage', as explained in Chapter 36). This basket makes the perfect gift, but it could also be used as a gift for anniversaries too.

What you need:

A basket – from a craft store or charity shop
Coloured ribbon
13 items that will all symbolise some aspect of the couple's relationship. Here are some examples:

Sun to represent the male
Moon to represent the female (if the relationship is two males then use two Suns, if it is two females use two Moons)
A dog figure for loyalty and protection
A cat figure for hearth and home
An owl for wisdom

A star for dreams
A clock to show that every moment counts
An acorn for strength
A toy car to represent their journey together
A small house to represent their home
A pinecone for prosperity
A heart for their love
A bee figure to representing accomplishing the impossible
A key to symbolise the opening of doors

Decorate the basket with the coloured ribbons, weaving them in and around the handle and the edges. Then you need to fill the basket with 13 items. You can add anything that you think represents the couple and their life together – be creative!

Sundial

An interesting project to make!

You will need:

- A stick. If you use a twig or branch make sure it is as straight as possible
- Several large stones
- A clock or watch so that you can calibrate the sundial

You need a spot in your garden that gets the most sun. Put the stick straight up into the earth. If you don't have a garden you could use a flowerpot filled with earth to put the stick in.

You will need to watch the clock now, at each hour place a stone where the shadow falls.

When all the daytime hours are marked your sundial is ready.

Litha meditation

Make yourself comfortable, close your eyes and focus on your breathing, deep breaths in… deep breaths out…

As your world around you dissipates you find yourself at the bottom of a grassy hill. It is dark but there is a pathway ahead of you that winds and spirals around the hill and it is lit with flaming torches so that you can find your way.

The air is warm but fresh. You breathe in the smell of the grass and the night air.

You start to make your way up the pathway. It is quite even but climbs steadily, spiralling around the grassy hill. You make your way up, up and up until as you near the top you see a tall stone tower standing magnificently on the top of the hill and cutting an imposing shape on the skyline and you realise you have just climbed the Tor in Glastonbury.

There are a few people seated around the base of the stone tower, all peaceful and relaxed, they are waiting for something...

One of them gestures for you to sit on the ground with them, offering you a blanket to sit on, which you do.

You make yourself comfortable and turn to face the direction that all the other people seem to be looking at. They are all watching the horizon.

Then you realise why... as the sun just makes itself known, breaking into the skyline with the first rays of the Summer Solstice. The sight takes your breath away, it is truly beautiful, such a magical feeling.

As the sun shows itself, those around you start to chant, a beautiful lilting sound that takes you with it, sending your senses reeling as you start to feel the magic around you.

You can feel the magic rising from the ground beneath you, it is the Summer Solstice and you are sitting on the underworld home of Gwyn App Nudd, King of the Faeries. Feel the energy rise as the magic of the fae meets the magic of the rays of the Summer Solstice Sun.

This energy creates a balance, one that you can draw from and use in your own life, in your own inner soul.

As the sun continues to rise the other people start to move and make ready to leave.

You send a blessing of thanks to the fae and start to ready yourself too.

Make your way back down the spiral pathway, winding back down the hill towards the place where you started your journey, taking the magical energy with you.

Slowly and gently bring yourself back to this reality.

Wriggling your fingers and toes and stretching your arms and legs, open your eyes.

Lughnasadh or Lammas

31st July/1st August

(Pronounced loo-nah-sah)

A time to celebrate the first harvest, we give thanks to the Earth for her bounty and beauty. Lughnasadh is associated with bread as grain is one of the first crops of the year to be harvested.

Corn dollies are symbolic for this festival. The figure of a maiden would be braided using the last harvested sheaf of grain to represent the spirit of harvest, and the doll would then be saved until the spring when it would be ploughed into the earth to ensure a good harvest. Sometimes the dolly is burnt in the Beltane fires to ensure abundance.

Symbols

Corn dollies, sun wheels, harvest tools, bread, cornucopias, sunflowers, sheaves of grain, sickles, scythes and herbs.

In the garden

The earlier summer flowing plants will be going over now, but there will still be plenty of colour. Keep watering and dead heading your flowers, saving and drying the petals and keep harvesting and drying the herbs.

Herbs

Corn, frankincense, heather, oak leaves, sunflowers and wheat.

Foods

Bread, corn, potatoes, nuts, wild berries, apples, rice, crab apples, squash, oats, grains, elderberry wine, ale and fruit pies.

Colours

Red, orange, yellow, green, brown and gold.

Activities

Baking homemade bread.

Spending time outside, making the most of the summer weather.

Organise a feast with your friends to celebrate the abundance that Mother Earth provides us with, get everyone to bring something they have made.

Meditate outside and give thanks for the abundance and prosperity of nature, on your own or with a group of friends. Leave an offering of bread.

Incense

Rose, rose hips, rosemary, chamomile, bay, coriander, meadowsweet, oregano, patchouli, frankincense, apple, heather and sandalwood.

Lammas incense recipe

Frankincense
Coriander
Meadowsweet
Oregano
Rosemary

Blend the ingredients together.

Oils

Basil, rose, heliotrope, hazelnut, sandalwood, oregano, rosemary, jasmine, bay and clove.

Lammas oil recipe 1

Blend together the following essential oils, with a base oil:

Hazelnut
Heliotrope
Basil
Rose

Lammas oil recipe 2

Blend together the following essential oils, with a base oil:

Sandalwood
Rose
Patchouli
Jasmine

Spell workings

Prosperity, abundance, good fortune, health, career and financial gain.

A fruitful spell

This is an edible spell (my favourite kind) and can involve the whole family or friends.

You will need a variety of fresh fruit to make a fruit salad such as:

Melon
Pineapple
Strawberries
Blueberries

Grapes
Oranges
Apples

As you start to clean and chop the fruit, focus on each type as you do so, adding it to a large bowl.

So as you chop the melon think about cutting up your money worries, visualise them disappearing.

Then with the pineapple, as you add the chunks to the bowl visualise each one being money that you add to your bank account.

For the strawberries, each one could be loose change that you find.

Grapes are good for abundance so as you add them to the bowl see them bringing abundance to you.

Blueberries are excellent for protection so add them to the bowl with the intent of protecting your spell.

Apples are also good for abundance so as you chop them and add them to the bowl visualise a healthy bank balance.

Oranges are good for luck and money so focus on this as you add them to the bowl.

When you are done, as you serve each person give them a blessing of abundance and prosperity. You could even have your guests say, 'So mote it be!' as a blessing of thanks.

Crafts

Berry bracelet

What you need:

Berries or hips – fresh or dried – experiment!
A needle
Cotton thread

Thread the needle then run the need through the stalks of the berries, or if the berries are dried or hard enough, through the berries themselves to make a bracelet. It might be a case of trial and error to find which way works best with which type of berries or hips. You can also add seeds or nuts as well. Give to a friend or a loved one.

Smudge sticks

If you have herbs growing in your garden then making your own smudge sticks is so easy.

What you need:

Lengths of herbs about 6in long such as lavender, rosemary or sage
Twine or string

Bunch the herbs together. You can use just one type or make a mixed bundle. I like to use the woody stems of the lavender plant when I cut it back mixed in with sprigs of sage, but go with what you have or what you prefer.

Tie them together at the base with the string, then wind the string up and around the bunch of herbs several times until it is all secure. Finish off with a knot to fix it all. Then leave it to dry.

Corn dolly

You will need:

Dried corn husks
Twine
Pens

Soak the husks in water until they become pliable. Then bunch together several of the husks and tie a piece of twine around them about half an inch from the end.

To form the head shape, hold by the tied end and one at a time fold the husks down over the twine. Tie another piece of twine around to create the neck.

To make the arms roll up one husk starting at the long edge, using twine to tie it off at both ends to form the wrists. Then fit the arms between the husks below the head and tie off to make a waist.

To make a skirt, use a couple more husks and tie them around the waist so that it looks like a skirt. For trousers separate the husk into two below the waist and tie each one at the ankle.

Then you can draw features on to make the faces and decorate with ribbon and fabric if you wish.

Bread dough wreath

What you need:

4 cups (33 oz) plain flour
1 cup (8 oz) salt
1 ½ cups (12 fl oz)warm water
Herbal tea bag

Steep the herbal tea bag in the warm water for a few minutes, then mix the flour and salt together and add the warm water. Mix well and knead until smooth.

Cover a baking sheet with aluminium foil and preheat the oven to 300F.

Take a large piece of the dough and roll it into a long sausage shape, then shape that into a circle and press the ends together. You might need a dab of water to make the ends stick.

Decorate the wreath as you like. Take small pieces of dough and flatten them and shape into leaves or flowers and add them to the circle of dough with a dab of water. You could also make fruit shapes adding cloves for detail.

When you have finished your design, bake it in the oven for

three hours until it is completely hard and dry. Leave it to cool.

To make the wreath last longer give it a coating of varnish (I use spray can varnish as it is quick and easy).

Lughnasadh meditation

Make yourself comfortable, close your eyes and focus on your breathing, deep breaths in… deep breaths out…

As your world around you dissipates you find yourself standing in a field of lush green grass and wild flowers. The air is warm, the sky is blue and the sun is shining. Around you butterflies and bees flit about hopping from flower to flower.

From where you are you have a wonderful view of the landscape around you, field upon field laid out before you like a huge patchwork quilt.

You sit down on the grass and make yourself comfortable. It is such a beautiful day and nature is positively brimming with life all around you.

The bees are collecting nectar to store away to make into honey, ever busy, ever industrious. You watch as one settles on a wild flower right next to you, so close you can hear the buzz. It collects the pollen, which adds to its already overloaded body, so covered in dusty yellow that it looks like the inside of a flower itself, then it flies off to the next flower, slightly clumsily as it is so heavily laden already.

In the field next to you are beautiful golden stalks of grain, swaying slightly in the late summer breeze.

In the field beyond that a combine harvester is cutting the grain ready to take away to store for the winter, the machine making stripy patterns in the field as it works its way around.

You notice a slight movement on the edge of the field just in front of you and look closer to see a small field mouse climbing up one of the stalks of grain. It stops as it hears a noise, still and quiet for a moment until it believes it has nothing to fear and then it carries on climbing. When it reaches the grain at the top it starts to eat, nibbling away at the seeds.

You look around the field you are sitting in, at all the beautiful wild flowers that Mother Nature has provided, the wonderful array of colours and the amazing scents that they carry with them.

A bird suddenly drops down on the fence post at the edge of the field in front of you, a black bird – he looks right at you and almost gives you a nod in greeting. He stops but for a moment and then he is off, soaring high up into the sky and heading for the trees.

You lay back in the grass and just stop for a moment, and listen – to the sounds of the machine collecting the harvest, the bees collecting pollen, the birds singing in the nearby trees, the sounds of late summer. You feel the warm sunshine on your face, and the slight breeze that brings the scent of the grass and the flowers with it. This is abundance, this is bounty, and these are the gifts of nature. Take a moment to be thankful for all that you have, send out a blessing.

When you are ready, sit up and take one last look around and then slowly and gently bring yourself back to your reality.

Wriggling your fingers and toes and stretching your arms and legs, open your eyes.

Southern Hemisphere

For those of you lovely people who reside in the Southern Hemisphere here is a list of the Sabbat dates for you:

Samhain: 30th April/1st May
Winter Solstice/Yule: 21st June
Imbolc: 2nd August
Ostara: 23rd September
Beltane: 31st October
Summer Solstice/Litha: 23rd December
Lughnasadh: 2nd February
Autumn Equinox/Mabon: 21st March

Chapter 45

Words in the Craft

When you first start out on this path you might come across some words that you find unfamiliar, just in case I have listed below some of the main ones (that possibly aren't covered in this book).

Amulet: A magically charged object but its purpose is to deflect and redirect energies independently even if the person is not holding or wearing it, it can be charged when the Moon is waning. An amulet works regardless of who is holding it or where it is left. For instance an amulet can be charged and left for years and still work.

Anointing oil: A skin-safe, sometimes scented, oil that is dabbed on the body (at chosen pulse points or on the forehead) in order to purify an individual mentally and spiritually.

Astral plane: A place that is generally thought of as an invisible parallel world which remains unseen from our own solid world of form.

Astral travel/projection: The process of separating your astral body from your physical one to accomplish travel in the astral plane or dream time.

Astrology: The study of and belief in the effects the movements and placements of planets and other heavenly bodies have on the lives and behaviour of human beings.

Banish: To magically end something or exorcise unwanted entities. To rid the presence of.

Book of Shadows: A witch's book of spells, rituals, magical lore, kind of a magical Bible or cook book, also called a grimoire.

Ceremonial magic: A highly codified magical tradition, often based upon Kabbala, the Jewish-Gnostic mystical teachings.

Channelling: A practice wherein you allow a discarnate entity to 'borrow' your body to speak to others either through automatic writing or verbally.

Charging: To infuse an object with personal power.

Charm: Either an amulet or talisman that has been charmed by saying an incantation over it and instilling it with energy for a specific task.

Circle: Sacred space wherein all magic is to be worked and all ritual contained. It both holds ritual energy until the witch is ready to release it, and provides protection for the witch.

Cone of power: Psychic energy raised and focused by either an individual or group mind (a coven) to achieve a definite purpose.

Coven: A group of witches who work together in an organised fashion for positive magical endeavours or to perform religious ceremonies.

Craft (The): Witchcraft

Dedication: The process where an individual accepts the Craft as their path and vows to study and learn all that is necessary to reach adept status. It is a conscious preparation to accept something new into your life and stick with it, regardless of the highs and lows that may follow.

Deity: Any supernatural being worshipped as controlling some part of the world or some aspect of life or who is the personification of a force. Divinity, God/dess, immortal.

Deosil: Clockwise, the direction in which the shadow on a sundial moves as the Sun 'moves' across the sky. Deosil is symbolic of life, positive magic, positive energies.

Divine power: The unmanifested, pure energy that exists within the Goddess and God. The life force, the ultimate source of all things.

Dowsing: The divinatory art of using a pendulum or stick to find the actual location of a person, place, thing, or element.

Drawing Down the Moon: A ritual performed during the Full Moon by witches to empower themselves and unite their essence with a particular deity, usually the Goddess.

Drawing Down the Sun: Companion ritual to Drawing Down the Moon in which the essence of the Sun God is drawn into the body of a male witch.

Duality: The opposite of polarity. When used as a religious term, it separates two opposites such as good and evil and places those characteristics into two completely separate God-forms.

Earth magic: The energy that exists within stones, herbs, flames, wind, and other natural objects.

Earth plane: Metaphor for your normal waking consciousness, or for the everyday, solid world we live in.

Evoke: To call forth within a particular space entities such as elementals or spirits, often to visible appearance.

Grimoire: A magical textbook, of which the Book of Shadows is an example

Grove: Synonymous with coven. Used mostly by Druids.

Guardians: Ceremonial magicians call the Guardians of the Watchtowers for the four quarters. Some witches use them, too.

Herbalism: Art of using herbs to facilitate human needs both magically and medicinally.

Initiation: A process whereby an individual is introduced or admitted into a coven. Usually a ritual occasion. Not to be confused with dedication.

Invocation: To bring something in from without.

Karma: The belief that one's thoughts and deeds can either be counted against them or added to their spiritual path across several lifetimes

Left-hand path: Refers to the practice of using magic to control others, to change the will of others, for personal gain. Generally frowned upon by true Wiccans and witches. Dark magic.

Libation: Ritually given portion of food or drink to a deity, nature spirit, or ghost.

Magic circle: A sphere constructed of personal power in which rituals are usually performed. Within it the witch is protected from outside forces. The sphere extends both above and below the surface of the ground.

Occult: Literal meaning is 'hidden' and is broadly applied to a wide range of metaphysical topics which lie outside the accepted realm of mainstream theologies.

Old Ones: The A term which refers to all aspects of the Goddess and God.

Old Religion: A name for paganism as it is indeed an incredibly old religion, pre-dating Christianity.

Pagan/neo-pagan: General term for followers of Wicca and other magical, shamanistic, and polytheistic Earth-based religions. The term pagan is also used to refer to pre-Christian religious and magical systems. Neo is the Greek word for 'new'.

Pantheon: A collection or group of Gods and Goddesses in a particular religious or mythical structure.

Pentacle: A circle surrounding a five-pointed, upright star (pentagram).

Pentagram: The basic interlaced five-pointed star, visualised with one point up. It represents the five elements: earth, air, fire, water, and spirit. It is a symbol of power and protection.

Personal power: The energy which sustains our bodies. It originates within the Goddess and God.

Polytheism: Belief in or worship of multiple deities, often assembled into pantheons.

Psychism: The act of being consciously psychic, in which the psychic mind and conscious mind are linked and working in harmony. Also known as psychic awareness.

Receptive or power hand: The hand through which energy is received into the body. Usually the left hand in right-handed persons, the reverse for left-handed persons but not always, go with what feels right for you.

Rede: The basic tenet of Wicca. 'An it harm none, do what thou will.' (This is one line from a longer version).

Reincarnation: The process of repeated incarnations in human (or sometimes animal) form to allow evolution of the soul.

Ritual tools: General name for magical tools used by a witch or magician.

Sabbats: Pagan celebrations for the Wheel of the Year festivities.

Sigil: Magically oriented seal, sign, glyph, or other device used in a magical working.

Skyclad: The act of celebrating or performing magical works in the nude.

Solitary: Pagan who works and worships alone.

Spiral: Symbol of coming into being.

Sympathetic magic: Concept of likes attracting each other.

Talisman: A magically charged object, the purpose of which is to attract energies. It can be charged when the Moon is waxing. It is an object that is made with the intent of creating change. Talismans work best with interaction from the person who holds them.

Threefold Law: Karmic principle that energy that is released is returned at least three times over.

Tradition: A type of paganism followed by a coven or grove.

Visualisation: The process of forming mental images. Magical visualisation consists of forming images of needed goals during ritual.

Warlock: An outdated term misused in reference to a male witch. It means oath-breaker or liar. Most pagans and witches don't use this term.

Wheel of the Year: One full cycle of the seasonal year.

Wicca: A modern religion with spiritual roots in paganism.

Widdershins: Counter-clockwise motion, usually used for negative magical purposes, or for dispersing negative energies.

Witch: A practitioner of folk magic, particularly that kind relating to herbs, stones, colours, etc. It is used by some Wiccans to describe themselves, but a witch isn't necessarily a Wiccan and vice versa.

Afterword: From Me to You

It has been wonderful to share my own Book of Shadows and experiences with you. I don't profess to know it all not by a long shot, I doubt I ever will. Learning is a long and exciting process and I think life would be pretty boring if there was nothing left to learn.

There is a saying that if you asked 13 witches the same question you would get 14 different answers. Every witch will work a slightly different way and will have slightly different ideas and views, that is part of what makes us human. I love that within witchcraft you can take it and make it your own. I encourage you to do so. If it feels right to you then go with your instinct… even if a book or the internet says different ;-)

Hopefully this book has gone someway to help you find your witch within…

With many blessings to you all.

MOON BOOKS

Moon Books invites you to begin or deepen your encounter with Paganism, in all its rich, creative, flourishing forms.

9781780999586